LEARNING FROM THE BOOK OF NATURE

By William Child

Artist: Barbara Child

Cover Artist: Lester Miller

ROD AND STAFF PUBLISHERS, INC.
Crockett, Kentucky 41413
Telephone: (606) 522-4348

Adapted from Companions, Christian Light Publications, Inc. Used by permission.

Chapter Four
"Solid Bedrock—Upheaval in Jim Walker's Pasture"

Chapter Five
"Life in a Forest—A Gopher, a Fungus, a Tree"

Chapter Eight
"Weeds—Thorns and Thistles"

Chapter Eleven
"Watersheds—The Continental Divide"

Chapter Nineteen
"The Sun and Its Light—Sunlight and Sonlight"

Copyright 1996
by
ROD AND STAFF PUBLISHERS, INC.
Crockett, Kentucky 41413

Printed in U.S.A.
ISBN 0-7399-0147-8
Catalog no. 2307

4 5 6 7 8 — 17 16 15 14 13 12 11 10 09 08

CONTENTS

Introduction

1. Nature Appreciation
   A Walk on a Fine Day in Fall 15
2. Parasites
   *Good Bumblebees and
      Bad Bumblebees* 23
3. Pines
   Job and the Monterey Pine 39
4. Solid Bedrock
   Upheaval in Jim Walker's Pasture ..47
5. Life in a Forest
   A Gopher, a Fungus, and a Tree 55
6. Tree Roots
   Sympathetic Roots 63
7. Forest Fires
   *Hard Seed, Pitchy Cones,
      and Drape* 69

8. Weeds
    Thorns and Thistles 85
9. Woodpeckers
    Red-Head and Scarlet-Crest 91
10. Animals and Tools
    *Not Hammers and Saws, But
        Tools Nonetheless* 105
11. Watersheds
    The Continental Divide 115
12. Camouflage and Mimicry
    Pretense 123
13. The North American Desert
    Hope 139
14. Insect Pests and Solenodon
    It Seemed Like a Good Idea 153
15. Ant, Hornbill, Salmon, and Beaver
    *Insects, Fowls, Beasts,
        and the Sluggard* 161

16. Alarming Occurrences
   Frightening Things Also Declare the Glory of God...................171

17. Adoption in Nature
   God the Father and Joseph the Father—of Jesus..............177

18. The Domestic Hen
   The Example of a Mother Hen....185

19. The Sun and Its Light
   The Ecology of the Universe Sunlight and Sonlight............195

INTRODUCTION

What do you think of when you look at nature? Do you think of God? If you do, you are thinking rightly, because God made it. Nature is God's creation. He created it for *us*.

First, God created nature to sustain us—to give us food, the materials we need for clothing, shelter, fuel, and all the other things we need to live.

Second, God created nature to inspire us. The psalmist said thousands of years ago, "The heavens declare the glory of God; and the firmament sheweth his handywork" (Psalm 19:1). Today there are still people who take their first step of faith toward God because they cannot ignore His work in nature, which testifies of a Creator—their Creator.

Genesis 2:9 is a wonderful verse near the beginning of the Bible that gives three reasons God created nature. Though this verse specifically mentions trees, I am sure the thought applies to nature in general.

The first two reasons Genesis 2:9 gives for God's creation are those mentioned above: inspiration and sustenance. "And out of the ground made the Lord God to grow every tree that is pleasant to the sight." Thus, at the start the Bible tells us that God created nature to inspire us. Next, this verse says that He made nature to sustain us: God made every tree that is "good for food." So when we look at nature, we can see God's love and His generosity.

But it is the third reason Genesis 2:9 gives for God creating nature that we will give most of our attention to in this book. God made "the tree of life also in the midst of the garden, and tree of the knowledge of good and evil." God created nature so that man could learn spiritual lessons from it. Rightly and reverently accepted as God's work, nature is indeed a source of spiritual lessons for mankind.

In all the works of God's creation, we can see and learn something of Him and His ways. This is true whether we look to the heavens above, at the thin shell occupied by life on the surface of the earth, or even into the rocky depths below our feet. We can learn something about God from plants and animals, whether we look at an entire assembly or at an individual organism.

The Book of Nature records something of God's character, His will, and His way, whether the chapter we read is written in a few square inches of lawn in our yard, in the depths of the sea, on the expanses of the land, or far into the seemingly limitless universe.

The inspiration for this book came from the Lord; the idea for the title came from page 23 of *Doctrines of the Bible* (Daniel Kauffman, editor; Herald Press, 1928). There it is explained that God is revealed to His children in four ways: in the Bible (the Book of Revelation); in creation (the Book of Nature); in the work of God in His people; and in Jesus Christ, the Word become flesh.

As we study God's creation, we must remember that the Book of Nature is someday to be forever closed—it is not eternal. God's Word is our most important study. God's Word *is* eternal; it will stand forever.

As you observe God's work in nature, avoid

the position of the casual observer. Remember that you are seeing part of His revelation of Himself, so as you look on, think of His wisdom. What would He have you learn from nature in its simplicity, intricacy, and variety? Do not be sidetracked by the theories and claims of men as to the *hows* and *whys*. The wisdom that the Creator has revealed for you in His creation will affirm His Word, and He will be revealed in both.

—William Child

Chapter 1

NATURE APPRECIATION

A Walk on a Fine Day in Fall

Who gets the most out of nature appreciation?

On a Sunday afternoon in late September my four-year-old son and I were walking along the country road that goes by our home on the Cumberland Plateau in eastern Tennessee, enjoying the beauty of God's creation. To his mother and me, it seems that he himself is one of the beautiful things of the creation.

From within the first stretch of woods along the road, we heard an occasional series of slaps and rattles as acorns of white and chestnut oaks fell to the earth through layers of leaves and branches. In the understory of the woods, dogwood leaves hinted red. Next to the road in the sunny margin of the woods, the past summer's display of the little pink flowers of the tick trefoils had faded, ripening into strings of triangular seedpods ready to catch a ride on any passing furry or clothed creature. Their pretty pink, the snowy white of yellow-centered oxeye daisies, and the bright orange of butterfly weed were now replaced by the soft white candelabra of thoroughwort, the warm yellow plumes of goldenrod, and the high-rising purple of ironweed.

In a swale where a culvert passed under the road stood a slippery elm, its leaves blotched brown by the struggles of another season of life. To its left leaned a black willow, whose pale green leaves would soon change quietly to yellow. Their lichen-splotched trunks were surrounded by purple-topped, lush grasses thriving on the abundant moisture of the swale. Across the road, though hardly noticeable now for the broad-leaved shrubs sharing its dry knoll, a head-high red cedar assured that a spot of green would remain among the browns and grays of winter.

Next, the road rose uphill to pass between open fields. Here lay a small triangular corner of abandoned meadow bounded by road, woods, and cropland, a piece impractically shaped for modern farming. There among the bluestem and bluegrass had sprung up pioneers preceding the return of oak and hickory to the old fields—mitten-leaved sassafras, now showing bright red leaves here and there on lower branches, red-crested smooth sumac, and domed, bronzy purple brambles of blackberry.

Past this island of transition between cultivated land and woodland, on the left-hand side of the road a catch crop of soybeans mown for hay was still lying in the field, emanating the sweet odor of productive farmland. On the right was land recently cleared of timber but not yet farmed, lately grown up in ragweed—unappealing to the eye were it not for the white and pink trumpets of the bindweed twining around and through the stems and leaves of these coarse weeds.

In the expanse of blue sky overhead not even one puffy cumulus cloud was present; only high, sparse mares' tails and thin herringbones. These could not cool the warmth cast across the land by the September sun.

On the shoulder of the road my little son

found the unmarred remains of a daintily patterned brown-and-yellow butterfly. This he carried carefully cradled in his hand so that he might later share something of his adventure with his mother.

The open shade of the young woodland beyond the fields sheltered wands of tufted, rose-purple blazing star and bluish purple downy lobelia, ranked among short, limby oaks and evergreen, ever-coned, scrubby Virginia pines. At my son's request we temporarily captured some of the beauty there by cutting a bough with cones off a pine and collecting sprigs of blazing star and downy lobelia.

The sycamore was ahead, with its great, broad leaves and hard green fruit ordinarily so interesting to a little boy. This time it was not so prominent for us because of the intensely (and prematurely) colored red maple next to it and the patch of fluffy mistflowers along the ditch bank next to the road. ("May we take some leaves and flowers to Mother?")

Then we turned around for home and Mother's good dinner, discussing the mighty leaps of the grasshoppers catapulting across our path; wondering where the woolly caterpillars hurrying over the pavement were going; taking into consideration whether the poison ivy vines climbing one of the utility poles along the road would die if they grew onto the power lines; deliberating over the dietary needs of Helen, the black-and-yellow Argiope whose spider web had been a focus of interest at our house for several weeks.

It seemed wonderful to be alive on that particular Lord's Day in September—to be a special creature in a very good creation.

*   *   *   *   *

Nature appreciation is not only for children—there is a place for it in the life of the Christian. "God saw every thing that he had made, and, behold, it was very good" (Genesis 1:31). Certainly a Christian wants to see things as God sees them.

Encouragement and *refreshment*—these two words help explain the experience of the writer of Psalm 104 as he reflected on God's creative work. To him, nature, though intriguing in itself, was a source of inspiration too, because God is its Maker and Sustainer. "Bless the Lord, O my soul. O Lord my God, thou art very great; thou art clothed with honour and majesty."

As Jesus taught His disciples how to live by faith in God, He drew their thoughts to pleasant scenes from nature. "Consider the lilies of the field." "Behold the fowls of the air." Had we been with Jesus that day in Galilee, we could have beheld the very birds He spoke of and considered the same flowery fields He did. Though that event was long ago, the appeal of these two illustrations from nature is universal, and the power in Jesus' words has not diminished. Rather, it has multiplied.

There is great deceit at large in the world today that would bias our thinking against God as Creator and Sustainer. May we pray to God for a correct perception of nature. For the openhearted, the Lord has continual inspiration and many lessons in His creation. See nature as *His* book.

"And God said, Let the earth bring forth grass, the herb yielding seed, and the fruit tree yielding fruit after his kind, whose seed is in itself, upon the earth: and it was so."

"And God saw everything that he had made, and, behold, it was very good."

Genesis 1:11, 31

Chapter 2

PARASITES

Good Bumblebees
and Bad Bumblebees

Is there anything good about parasites?

From early in my childhood, the bumblebee has been one of my favorite creatures. As a boy I often paused to watch these rotund, deliberate insects clad in fuzzy yellow-and-black coats go slowly, thoroughly about their searches among the flowers and shrubs around our home. I have a clear mental picture of them collecting food from the broad, open blossoms of the stately hollyhocks growing atop the old coal clinker pile behind our house, flying from flower to flower, dusty with pollen. To me they are a symbol of spring and summer days. Today the heavy hum of a bumblebee in flight—often heard before it is seen—brings to mind gentle scenes from the past: green gooseberry bushes standing in the warm stillness of sun-drenched bluegrass pastures encircled by oak and hickory woodlands.

My feeling of affection for these easygoing members of the bumblebee family was not threatened even by the possibility that they could sting. After all, they never bothered me. (But maybe that was because I never bothered them.) And everything considered, when I learned that according to scientific principles it should be impossible for so portly an insect—with such a small set of wings—to fly, my appreciation for bumblebees only increased.

The time came, however, when I had to reevaluate my attitudes toward bumblebees. As an adult I learned that there is more than one kind of bumblebee, and that not all kinds are *my* kind.

The bumblebees that I have learned to appreciate are classified among those called *Bombus,* and, as I had always thought, they go about their work with slow industry in comparison with the hurrying honeybee, fulfilling their role in the creation without giving offense to anything else. Only the queen bumblebee survives over winter, and in the spring she comes forth from shelter in the ground to gather nectar and pollen from flowers, find a hole in the ground to use for a nest, and therein lay and incubate eggs. Thus a queen bee begins a new colony and maintains the order that God established in the first week of time—an order that assures the continuation of its own kind, as He has planned. Yes, this is labor that I could appreciate, always done according to the pattern that the Lord devised.

On the other hand, another group of bumblebees of which I learned, named *Psithyrus*, was not, in my opinion, at all to be admired. Unlike *Bombus,* it does not gather pollen or locate a nest of its own to build up a colony. It does not have to, because the *Psithyrus* queen tracks down the nest hole of a *Bombus* queen and lays her eggs therein for the *Bombus* workers to care for. Some *Psithyrus* queens take over the nest, stinging the *Bombus* queen to death and destroying her eggs so that there is no competition with the *Psithyrus* offspring for the attention of the *Bombus* workers.

My first reaction on learning of the way that *Psithyus* makes its living was disgust, but when I expressed my feelings to my wife, she reminded me that *Psithyrus*, like *Bombus*, is a creature of God's handiwork, and she admonished me that I should not disdain any of His work. Well said and well taken, this caused me to think further on a subject that I, along with countless others through the ages, have puzzled over.

A few months ago our small daughter expressed her own bewilderment over the same puzzle in this way: "Why did God make mosquitoes?" From a larger context, I have wondered, "Why did God create parasites?"

Understand me—as I ask this question today I am not questioning God's wisdom. What He created *is* to His glory. Since we look through a glass, darkly, we may not see how parasitic organisms fit into His glorious plan *now,* but someday the Christian will be able to understand. (Whether or not we will be *concerned* any longer about that kind of question when we at last see the Saviour face to face is another question.) However, the question "Why parasites?" is still a question worthy of consideration because, I believe, the part of the answer, or answers, we *can* now comprehend can be to our upbuilding in reverencing the Creator and in appreciating His creative work.

Our desire is to find spiritual lessons from the existence and influence of parasites. To do so, we will first consider their significance in God's natural creation. Second, we must look at the meaning of the weakness and disease sometimes resulting from extreme infestations of parasites. Finally, we will draw from parasitism insights into God's work in redeeming man.

**PARASITES
AND THE BALANCE OF NATURE**

Does it surprise you to think of creatures such as the *Psithyrus* bumblebee as parasites? The strict and limited definition of *parasite* that many of us have learned stays with us: a parasite is an organism living on or in another, taking its nourishment at the expense of its host. Most of us, when we hear the word parasite, picture strange, repulsive-looking creatures that are unwelcome inhabitants of the bodies of man and animals, such as tapeworms, roundworms, and flukes. As our mental picture enlarges, we may remember that some fungi and microscopic organisms, such as some disease-causing bacteria and protozoans, are parasites of man, animals, and plants. Further, we may think of aphids, mites, ticks, lice, mosquitoes, flies, and other crawling creatures that are parasites.

However, there are more complex methods of parasitism. Among birds there are such intruders as the brown-headed cowbird and several kinds of cuckoos. These are *brood* parasites, laying their eggs in the nests of smaller birds, who incubate these foreign eggs and feed the oversized nestlings—to the detriment of their own young. The parasitism that was described earlier of one kind of bumblebee by another may be classed with either brood parasitism or social parasitism.

To answer the question "What good are parasites?" in the natural sense, we may begin by asking another question: "What would happen without them?"

The most obvious effect of the absence of parasites would be improved health and increased reproduction of plants and animals ordinarily weakened or killed by parasites. There is a tremendous reproductive potential of various forms of life if natural controls are lacking. Without natural controls, one kind of plant or animal can come to the point of overpopulation, where its environment may not be able to support it and other kinds of organisms around it. Parasites are an important part of God's system of natural controls to maintain a balance in nature.

For those of you who, like me, are inclined to be bothered by such pesky creatures as the *Psithyrus* bumblebee, remember that it would be destructive to *Psithyrus's* own existence to kill off all *Bombus* bumblebees. *Psithyrus* needs *Bombus* to continue to multiply its own kind—*Psithyrus* would not "know" how to live without *Bombus*. We can trust in the balance of God's design to keep the populations of *Bombus* and *Psithyrus* at the levels needed to maintain healthy stocks of both.

In many parasite-host relationships, the population and effects of the parasite on (or in) the host stay at a level tolerable to the host until stress of some kind weakens the host. Then the infestation can increase to an intolerable level, severely weakening or killing the host. (See next chapter, "Job and the Monterey Pine.") Such an effect, though it may cause concern to *us*, can still be understood in terms of balance in the creation—the Creator has set ecological zones that may not be violated and natural limits that may not be exceeded without destroying this balance.

PARASITES OUT OF BALANCE

While the importance of parasitism in the balance of nature is apparent, still we must acknowledge that there are many troubling times when populations of parasites themselves get out of balance. The effects of these imbalances are inconvenient at best and disastrous at worst. It is difficult to pass over such devastating effects of parasites as malaria, dysentery, elephantiasis, sleeping sickness, and the Black Death as mere outworkings of the balance of nature.

To understand the causes of such intensive infestations of parasites, we can look to the Bible and what it tells us of the history of man and his relationship with God.

We have already emphasized the *balance of nature.* This is an easily observable fact: God *did* create a balanced system. However, there was an event in history that brought imbalance into this system, and since that time, "we know that the whole creation groaneth and travaileth in pain" (Romans 8:22).

That event was the willful disobedience of man against his Creator, who then cursed the ground for man's sake (Genesis 3). However, it is not only through the "thorns and thistles" among his crops that man experiences the curse God has given for his prideful resistance to the Holy One. Nature at large witnesses to the curse, and the environmental degradation that so much alarms men today is merely heightened evidence of the strivings of man against the balanced system in which the Lord placed Adam. Thus in nature the *imbalance* initiated through man's rejection of the Word of God *strives* against the *balance* established by Him.

It is in terms of the imbalance introduced into the creation through man's sin that the weakening and sometimes ravaging effects of parasites on man and his surroundings must be understood. With our time-bound perceptions, we cannot know in detail what life was like for man before God pronounced the curse upon him and the earth because of Adam's sin. Neither can we know what God's plan for the creatures we call parasites was before the Fall; but we do know from God's Word that man's sin affected the whole creation, and that includes the parasites.

Man was intended to live in a fruitful garden "to dress it and to keep it" (Genesis 2:15). He now lives in houses, and the great majority of mankind is concentrated in cities. Man's parasites are housed and concentrated with him. Likewise, his livestock, created by God with instincts that would cause them to avoid severe infestations of parasites by moving around and seeking food and shelter over an area large enough for their natural needs, are concentrated on pastures, on feedlots, and in buildings. Also, his crops are planted as enormous, close-growing populations of the same kind of plants, an arrangement conducive to rampant damage by parasites.

Contrast this to the great diversity of plants found naturally on wildlands. Natural ecosystems have plant populations created by God with the capability to undergo the recurring effects of parasites yet stay in balance.

We may think of exceptions to balanced parasitism in wildlands. However, if we search into the case, we find the influence of man somewhere in starting the problem or in making an existing situation worse. Consider these three examples.

1. The chestnut blight, which killed most of the American chestnut trees in North America, was caused by a fungal parasite. However, the fungus probably came to the United States from Japan in the late 1800s. Chestnut blight comes

from a disease-causing parasite that is out of place through men's activities, living on a host not designed to survive its attack.

2. Wildlife populations in an area may be greatly reduced or devastated by parasites. In such an instance, ask these questions: How far away were man's pets and livestock? Did they introduce or at least help to spread the problem?

3. As the forests in the Great Lakes states changed following settlement, Kirtland's warbler was headed toward extinction. After its need for certain types of forest cover was learned and government agencies began to manage their lands in ways to help the warbler population recover, it was recognized that brood parasitism by the brown-headed cowbird was another major problem. So the government workers began trapping cowbirds, thus helping to increase the warbler population. How was the cowbird problem initiated? Cowbirds had moved into the area with the farmers (and their cows), parasitizing a little bird that was not created with the instincts to overcome their crafty behavior. (If some other kinds of warblers discover a cowbird egg in their nests, they will build a new nest on top of the first one.)

PARASITES AND GOD'S WORK IN THE REDEMPTION OF MAN

As we have seen, the creatures we call parasites have an important continuing role in maintaining balance in God's natural creation. However, their most weakening and destructive influences are two of the effects of an imbalance introduced into the world by man's rejection of God's Word. The role of parasites in maintaining natural balance in God's orderly world contrasts with their more intensely harmful effects resulting from imbalance in creation due to man's sin. There are lessons about God's unfolding work in the redemption of man in these contrasting works of parasites.

Man is a vessel of clay that should be filled with humility (Isaiah 64:8; Micah 6:8). Our boast should be in the Lord. We should have no pride in ourselves (Romans 3:10–12; Psalm 34:2). Satan aimed at God through man's pride when he tempted Eve in the Garden. The desire of the first man and woman to step above their place in God's order brought the curse that was necessary to humble them. This curse was an act of our loving and just God that was necessary to open a

Parasites

gate through which man can reenter into fellowship with Him.

To enter the kingdom of heaven today, we still must become humble before God. Pride brings resistance from the Lord (James 4:6), and the curse is still the same. The curse is a humbling influence to help make proud man see his own need for salvation and look to God for redemption through Jesus Christ.

We are still cursed with the weeds in our crops as God promised Adam, but the thorns and thistles of Genesis 3:17–19 may be understood figuratively, as well as literally. Besides weeds, there is a long list of natural influences that should help us to know our vulnerable, temporary status as creatures of flesh: insect pests, hail, winds, storms, flood, drought, disease, and *parasites* name a partial list. Man is indeed a vessel of clay whose greatest works fade away. The parasites that trouble him, his livestock, and his crops should be helpful reminders to him of his own weakness.

Man's efforts to ultimately control his environment are futile. Each new effort brings large-scale problems in another area. Witness the side effects of some of the methods that man has developed to reduce the labor needed to raise crops: pollution by pesticides, herbicides, and chemical fertilizers only adds to the pollution from urban and industrial sources. Like his unending battle with weeds that compete with his crops, man will continue to experience the problems caused by parasites as long as the earth abides.

The earth will abide until after Jesus reigns as King of kings at the final judgment of mankind. Then, for those bound for heaven, "there shall be no more curse" and there will be no more strife. Eternal balance will be restored—then thorns, thistles, *and* parasites will be no more (Revelation 20–22).

"As for God, his way is perfect: the way of the Lord is tried: he is a buckler to all those that trust in him.

"For who is God save the Lord? or who is a rock save our God?

"It is God that girdeth me with strength, and maketh my way perfect."

Psalm 18:30–32

Chapter 3

PINES

Job and the Monterey Pine

If enough stress is applied, will it always destroy?

We will travel to New Zealand, an island country about twelve hundred miles southeast of Australia. Here we will study the Monterey pine and its response to several kinds of *stresses* that are physical hardships for the tree. Then we will look at the Bible account of Job's response to stresses in his life. This comparison of things as different as the lives of Job and the Monterey pine can teach us important lessons about God's plan for mankind.

The Monterey pine is a rare tree in its native California. While not native to New Zealand—no pines are native to the Southern Hemisphere—it is the most common pine in forest plantations there.

A problem for the growth of Monterey pines in New Zealand is that they are attacked in unusually wet years by soil fungi. A fungus is a type of nongreen plant. That is, it does not have chlorophyll as green plants have. Since chlorophyll is necessary to a plant for food production, a fungus cannot make its own food. Some fungi get their food from dead plants or animals, but others attack living plants or animals.

One example of fungi is the kind that produces toadstools. The toadstool is really only the fruit of an underground fungus. A toadstool puts off tiny bodies, termed *spores*, that fall to the ground to reproduce more fungi. The toadstool arises from the main body of the fungus, which lies underground.

The type of fungus we are considering here destroys the tiny feeder roots of the Monterey pine. It is a *parasite*. It slowly kills the plant that it depends upon for its food. This attack is at its worst in very wet years. If a normally moist year follows the wet year, the Monterey pine may restore part of its root system. If this happens, it has recovered from the stress that could have killed it.

Like all living things, the Monterey pine has more than one enemy to its health. Another of its enemies is the immature form, or *larva,* of the wood wasp. This insect's larva, a parasite, eats the cells of the growing tissue, the *cambium,* of the pine, and is a serious threat to the tree in dry years, when moisture stress is at its worst.

Do you see what will happen to a Monterey pine in New Zealand when a dry period follows an unusually wet year? In a wet year the fungi destroy the feeder roots. The tree's ability to absorb water and minerals from the soil is therefore severely reduced. If dry years follow when there is little moisture in the soil, even more moisture stress comes to the pine, as there are too few rootlets to absorb the limited moisture that is there. The weakened tree is then attacked by the wood wasp, which lays its eggs under the bark of the pine. The larvae that hatch eat the growing tissue, the cambium. The result is death to the tree.

Let us picture this sequence in our minds in

the way a chemist writes an equation for a chemical reaction.

$$\text{Monterey Pine} + \text{Fungi (in wet year)} + \text{Wood Wasp (in dry year)} \longrightarrow \text{Dead Tree}$$

This shows that if a healthy tree is weakened by soil fungi in a wet year, a wood wasp attack in a succeeding dry year will yield a dead tree.

In the Old Testament we read of the experience of Job. Job was a man "perfect and upright" (Job 1:1). Most important, he was spiritually healthy—he "feared God, and eschewed evil" (Job 1:1). In the prime of his life he came under close attack by Satan. He was put under stresses that would have destroyed most men. Indeed, this was Satan's plan. Through stresses in Job's earthly life, Satan hoped to destroy his faith in God. Then Job would be separated from God forever.

At least, this was Satan's intention. However, he did not count on the strength to endure hardship that comes to the faithful believer in the one true God.

First, Job lost his possessions. Next, all his children died at once in a catastrophe. After this, disease struck him. As though these disasters were not enough, his wife tried to discourage him. "Then said his wife unto him, . . . curse God, and die. But he said unto her, Thou speakest as one of the foolish women speaketh. What? shall we receive good at the hand of God, and shall we not receive evil? In all this did not Job sin with his lips" (Job 2:9, 10). Finally, even his friends came and belittled him.

As with plants and animals, stress can weaken man so much that death results. In physical life we see this happening following disease, accident, hunger, thirst, and so on. For man there is another, more important, area open to stress—the spiritual life. This is the part of Job that Satan wanted to destroy. Satan thought that sufficient stress would destroy Job's faith. However, Job's faith in God stayed strong. He was able to say to God after all his trials: "I have heard of thee by the hearing of the ear: but now mine eye seeth thee" (Job 42:5).

Let us picture Job's trial and his triumph like a chemical equation, as we did for stresses and death in the pine.

LEARNING FROM THE BOOK OF NATURE

$$\text{Job + Loss of Wealth and Children + Loss of Health + Discouragement by Wife + Belittling by Friends} \xrightarrow{\text{Faith in God}} \text{Victory for Job}$$

No doubt you have noticed a difference in the basic form of the two equations. The one for Job has "Faith in God" written over the arrow. In chemistry oftentimes there is something required to make the process (a chemical reaction) work quickly, but this "something" is not used up or destroyed in the process: it is the same after the process is completed as it was at the beginning. This is called a *catalyst*. When the name of the catalyst is written in the chemical equation, it is placed on the arrow. An everyday example is:

$$\text{Starch} \xrightarrow{\textit{Amylase}} \text{Sugars}$$

This is the process needed for the digestion of starchy foods by plants, animals, and man. Amylase must be present to digest the starch into sugar, but it is not changed in the process. It is a catalyst and can be used again.

Faith in God made Job victorious over the

stresses of life. Like a catalyst in a chemical reaction, his faith was undiminished and unchanged by the process. Job was still trusting God after the severe stresses were gone.

Victory through faith is God's desire for all mankind. When a pine, a fungus, a wood wasp, or any other plant or animal dies, it is dead forever, but as for man, "whoso putteth his trust in the Lord shall be safe" (Proverbs 29:25). He shall live forever.

Chapter 4

SOLID BEDROCK

Upheaval in
Jim Walker's Pasture

What is God telling us through the order He established in nature?

In the spring of 1973, residents of the area around Elk City saw a startling addition to their western Oklahoma landscape.

In a pasture on Jim Walker's ranch, an upheaval in the shale bedrock that underlies the region threw up a craggy wall of red stones. The stones thrust up as high as twenty feet and weighed as much as thirty tons. These massive boulders littered more than half an acre. Deep, narrow cracks fissured the earth around the jagged wall. Trees and shrubs that had been uprooted sprawled across the ground.

Debate over the possible cause of the upheaval ranged from terrestrial forces, such as an earthquake, to the extraterrestrial, such as a large meteor. However, scientists from the Oklahoma Geological Survey soon discovered the real reason for the strange rock pile in Jim Walker's pasture.

In 1953 an oil company had drilled a well about two-fifths of a mile north of this location. At a depth of thirteen hundred feet, drilling was stopped at a salt bed. However, the dry hole was used to inject propane into the earth for storage. The well casing was apparently unsound, and the gas leaked into the surrounding rock. At last pressure built up beyond the ability of the earth's crust to resist. The red shales of the Oklahoma plains had to yield.

This is an unusual case where man has forced material into the earth's crust and caused a relatively small disturbance at the surface. Examples of surface disturbances that result from the removal of minerals below the surface are much more common. Slow sinking and even sudden collapse of the earth's surface occurs in the coal mining districts of Pennsylvania.

Solid Bedrock

Even removal of ground water for man's purposes has caused areas of the earth's surface to settle or sink. Before Europeans saw Mexico City, land drainage was already causing the land around the city to sink. As time passed and the city grew, pumping of water from the earth for urban use accelerated the sinking.

Commenting on the upheaval in Jim Walker's pasture, someone expressed the thought that man's interference with "earth's natural order" resulted in an unexpected geological disturbance.

We can thank God for the revelation in His Word that He is the author of this order in the natural world. This revelation helps Christians to see that the calamities man brings on himself through interference with God's natural order are evidence that God is the Creator and His natural laws cannot be altered.

Often we experience, observe, or hear of examples in which man has interfered with or attempted to ignore God's natural laws. Ignoring God's natural laws may be costly, disastrous, or even deadly. The driver of an automobile enters a curve on a wooded road at a rate of speed exceeding the capability of the tires to maintain a rolling friction with the road surface.

LEARNING FROM THE BOOK OF NATURE

A skid results. The vehicle leaves the road. A powerful force meets a stationary object, and tragedy occurs.

There is also a spiritual order in God's creation that must not be violated. The spiritual order God designed for His creation is outlined in the Bible. It is an order affecting all who have ever lived (Acts 17:24–31). It applies even after death (2 Timothy 4:1; Revelation 20:12–15). To reject it is even more perilous than attempting to ignore God's natural laws (Matthew 18:7–9).

While this order applies especially to each of us individually, God has planned that the church be a model, or example, of how His spiritual order should be applied in the world of men. Through the church, God and His spiritual order are continually to be held up before man until Christ returns (Matthew 5:13–16).

Just as man's violation of God's natural laws often brings disaster, so no man or woman or boy or girl can contradict God's spiritual order without causing a disastrous effect sooner or later. No matter if the violation seems small; the effect can still be great (Romans 14:1–21; 1 Corinthians 8:9). Christians must, therefore, consider every decision and action in light of its effects in

Solid Bedrock

their own lives, the lives of others, and the lives of those yet unborn.

To illustrate, our Christian brothers and sisters in our church fellowship are sufficiently submitted together as members of the body of Christ that agreement has been reached on standards on motor vehicles, home furnishings, dress, and so on. They have deep concern and consideration for one another and for each one's personal as well as their combined witness to the world. This shows even in the ordinary things of life. Praise God that He can guide faithful congregations into such unity!

That dress or shirt, that wall motto, that car or truck—will it contribute faithfully to the standards of witness we have agreed to accept, or does it push the limits? Or even worse, is it in direct violation of the standards of witness we have promised our brothers and sisters in Christ that we will help to maintain?

What current and long-range effects does pushing or exceeding the limit in so-called small things have on the big things? Do any among us believe that offense to the agreed-to order of the church in "small things" will not have damaging and disastrous effects in terms of the salvation of souls? Notice the strong words of Jesus for the person who causes a believer in Christ to stumble (Matthew 18:1–7).

God's order in nature is intended to help convince men that the spiritual order revealed in His Word is true (Romans 1:20). There is no order to follow that will keep us faithful to Christ other than the order of Christ as outlined in the Word. Let us be quick to follow Christ when He speaks to us of God's order through the church.

"Blessed is the man that walketh not in the counsel of the ungodly, nor standeth in the way of sinners, nor sitteth in the seat of the scornful.

"But his delight is in the law of the Lord; and in his law doth he meditate day and night.

"And he shall be like a tree planted by the rivers of water, that bringeth forth his fruit in his season; his leaf also shall not whither; and whatsoever he doeth shall prosper."

Psalm 1:1–3

Chapter 5

LIFE IN A FOREST

A Gopher, a Fungus, and a Tree

How is a forest like the church?

"The heavens declare the glory of God; and the firmament sheweth his handywork" (Psalm 19:1).

Gazing into the heavens on a starry night, people often speak of belief in an eternal Creator. To those who pause to look, the exquisite beauty of a flower, a butterfly, a tree in fall color, or a sunset shows the power of the Designer in His creation. Just as the Bible gives new insights into God's ways and means each time we read it, so God has provided in nature a seemingly limitless source of lessons to illustrate for all men the

LEARNING FROM THE BOOK OF NATURE

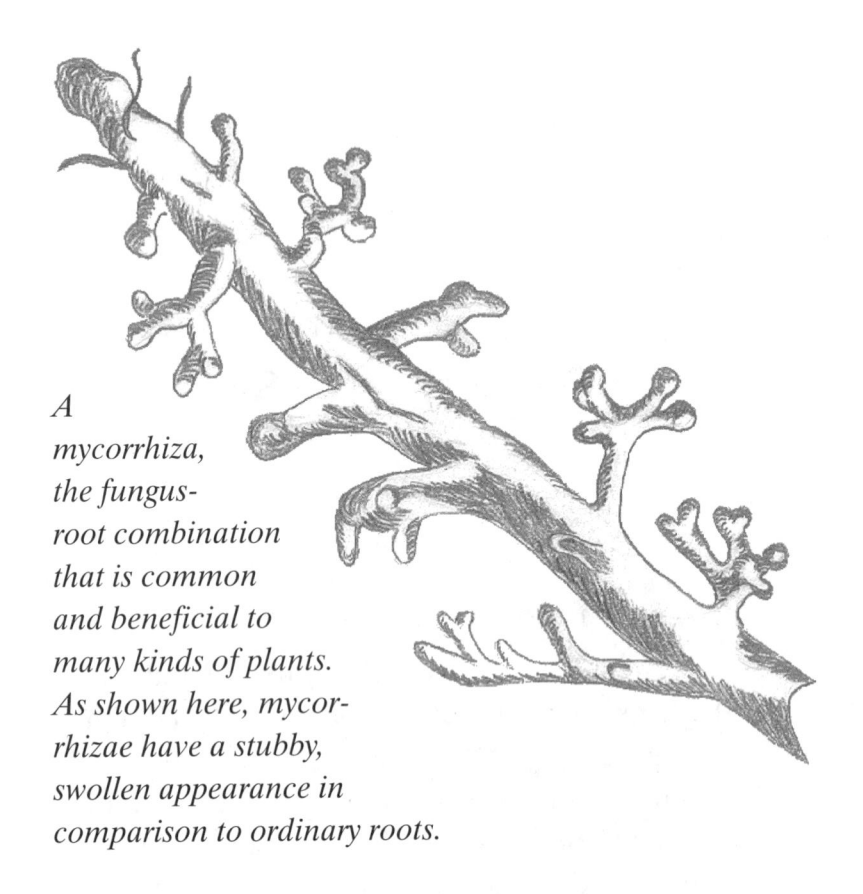

A mycorrhiza, the fungus-root combination that is common and beneficial to many kinds of plants. As shown here, mycorrhizae have a stubby, swollen appearance in comparison to ordinary roots.

authenticity of the Scriptures.

One such lesson can be learned from the interdependent relationship of forest trees with some kinds of soil fungi. The fine tree roots and the fungi intermingle. This intermingling forms masses called *mycorrhizae*. The fungus helps the tree to get food from the soil that it could not get otherwise, and the fungus in turn receives part of the food that the tree makes.

These mutual benefits are such an established part of life in the forest that trees and fungi both thrive in one another's presence, but each would live more meagerly if on its own. In fact, soil in forest tree nurseries often must be inoculated with the fungi that form mycorrhizae with the kinds of trees being grown, or the business of propagation is bound to fail. This has also been true with the extensive plantings of Monterey pine and other conifers in the Southern Hemisphere, referred to in "Job and the Monterey Pine" (Chapter 3 in this book). When the pines were introduced south of the equator, their complementary mycorrhizae-forming fungi had to be taken along too.

Soil fungi are best known for the mushrooms and the toadstools that some of them push above the ground. These are the parts of the fungi that produce tiny spores that drift through the air, settle on the soil, and reproduce their own kind.

However, some of the most common soil fungi that form mycorrhizae on tree roots do not produce mushrooms or toadstools. Therefore they are not able to place their spores above ground to spread and reproduce their own kind. Yet the forest trees must have these cooperative fungi in order to survive and to colonize new areas. What is the answer to this seemingly natural impasse?

God provided the answer through the interrelationships He created among the plants and animals that dwell in the forest. Animals such as gophers dig up the fungi when the spores are ripe. The odor of the fungi reaches a peak at this time; therefore the animals have no trouble sniffing them out. They excavate the fungi from the ground and eat them. Their excrement then contains the fungal spores and is scattered over the land. The spread of the soil fungi is thus assured.

God has provided a balanced, interdependent relationship in the forest to assure growth, reproduction, and spread of trees, soil fungi, and gophers.

In the church the Lord has given His children an environment in which they can grow to spiritual maturity, bear spiritual fruit in this life, and attain to eternal life in the world hereafter. The church is the body of Christ, whose functioning Paul describes in 1 Corinthians 12.

Growth of pine seedlings is faster and healthier when mycorrhizae-forming fungi are present. The seedling on the right benefited from mycorrhizal roots. The one on the left is the same age but grew without mycorrhizae-forming fungi.

LEARNING FROM THE BOOK OF NATURE

How would it be if the forest were only trees, or if the body "were all one member" (verse 19)? What if the tree would say to the gopher and fungus, or the eye to the hand, "I have no need of thee" (verse 21)?

No, in the forest—indeed, in all of nature—and in the church "those members of the body, which seem to be more feeble, are necessary" (verse 22). In the forest there is not schism between tree, animal, and fungus. Similarily, in the body of Christ "there should be no schism . . . but that the members should have the same care one for another" (verse 25).

The Lord's creation will always glorify Him and provide inspiration and instruction for His children. "For the invisible things of him from the creation of the world are clearly seen, being understood by the things that are made, even his eternal power and Godhead; so that they are without excuse" (Romans 1:20).

"But now hath God set the members every one of them in the body, as it hath pleased him. . . .

"And the eye cannot say unto the hand, I have no need of thee: nor again the head to the feet, I have no need of you.

"Nay, much more those members of the body, which seem to be more feeble, are necessary. . . .

"Now ye are the body of Christ, and members in particular."

1 Corinthians 12:18, 21, 22, 27

Chapter 6

TREE ROOTS

Sympathetic Roots

Did you know that God made trees that can help one another?

"And if some of the branches be broken off, and thou, being a wild olive tree, wert graffed in among them, and with them partakest of the root and fatness of the olive tree; boast not against the branches. But if thou boast, thou bearest not the root, but the root thee" (Romans 11:17, 18).

In these verses the apostle Paul illustrated our union with the people of God in a way that those in an agricultural society could understand. When we who were not born of the children of Israel believe in the one true God, we are "graffed" onto their "tree" and share in God's covenant with them.

But the Bible was written for people in every society and age. Today we can draw further insights from this example of the graft union of a Gentile believer with the body of Christ. The Word of God is ever fresh.

Ecologists have found that many trees in the forest form root grafts with others of the same kind. Through these root grafts, trees pass food and water and even diseases to one another.

Even under very extreme conditions, the sharing of food and water continues through root grafts. Stumps of some kinds of trees have been known to continue to grow in diameter without resprouting for ten to twenty years after their tops have been cut off. Sometimes the stumps even grow in diameter faster than the trees that are supplying them through the root grafts.

What happens to these fruitless, dependent stumps in the next round of logging when the trees that supply them are cut down? Must they die and decay at last? Not necessarily.

After years of receiving food and water from their neighboring nurse trees, when these trees are cut down, the old stump may resprout, and produce a new growth of leaves and branches. The stump then changes from a recipient of the forest's welfare to a producer for the forest's benefit.

Root grafts do not always serve to the advantage of the trees. The disappearance of the American elms that graced our city streets and countryside years ago was sped up as Dutch elm disease was passed from infected trees to healthy ones through root grafts. The occasional American elms that are still alive are free-standing trees that are less subject to attack by the beetle that carries the disease and are not united with other elms by root grafts.

How very like the interdependence of these root-grafted trees is that of the Christian to other believers in the church. Spiritual food and water are not merely kept by the individual believer but will be passed on, through him or her, to others in the body of Christ. As in the example of root-grafted trees, the purpose is not to increase the one and decrease the other, but that both can grow into "trees" that glorify the Creator.

There is also an admonition in this illustration from nature. As with the disease that can pass by root grafts from one tree to another, so spiritual illness can be transmitted from one believer to another. Praise God for a prescription that can control this disease and cleanse us from its effects! This is the spiritual medicine of the written Word, applied under the guidance of God's Holy Spirit.

What is there to be learned from this illustration of the root graft for those of us who are like the stumps? We may have spent the early years of our lives not in service to God but in service to His enemy. Surely we are like stumps in that the strength of our youth has been cut off.

Then we turn to the Master, who is able to do all things. In His power we are born again in newness of life. This New Birth means we begin to grow in Christ. God has provided several sources of spiritual food to nurture our growth. One source is His written Word, the Holy Bible. Another source is His Holy Spirit at work in our hearts. A third source—the one we want to emphasize here—is His church, made up of fellow believers attaining to the holiness of Christ.

God made the trees of the forest to form root grafts that allow them to share with each other. How much more is He able and willing to form between us and His other children a union that can transmit spiritual food and water! Then, even as "stumps," we receive help from other growing Christians that we might grow in spirit too.

But as is characteristic of so great a God, there is more. We are not left to an existence as dependent "stumps." Through the continuing nourishment of the Scriptures, the Holy Spirit in our hearts, and the church, we can grow new "branches" and new "leaves." Then we can go on as full participants in the body of believers as it provides spiritual food for a growing church and a needy world.

Chapter 7

FOREST FIRES

Hard Seed, Pitchy Cones, and Drape

Can there be anything like a "good" forest fire?

The government has had such an effective anti-forest fire program that it is difficult for people to think of a forest fire as anything but an enemy. But not all forest fires are bad. The fact is, fire is a natural and necessary part of the life cycle of most types of wildlands.

THE IMPORTANCE OF FIRE TO WILDLANDS

Fire is a force God has provided to help maintain the natural diversity that is so pleasing in His creation. That diversity is, in part, a measure of a healthy environment.

Without fire, forests and grasslands become somewhat like cornfields; and without fire they have some of the same problems as cornfields. For example, there are continual insect and disease problems, and often they are not able to reproduce themselves without intensive management.

Further, forests and grasslands that lack in diversity have some problems of their own, such as a buildup of fuels (living and dead burnable materials) to the extent that any fire that does occur has the potential to become a holocaust. Does this sound familiar? It might, for this is the situation often faced in forest and range management today.

Forest and range management has of necessity become much more intensive and costly than men would have believed possible just a few decades ago. As costs have risen and the health of range and forestlands has continued to decline, managers have reevaluated their management techniques. One tool they have rediscovered is fire.

Today fire is being *prescribed* for wildlands.

Forest Fires

That is, land managers examine an area and then prescribe a certain kind of controlled burn if one is needed. If an area has become environmentally unhealthy, the fire they prescribe is planned so that it will burn at the proper intensity to improve its health. When an area has come under improved management (including fire management), then fire is prescribed to maintain its health.

Benefits of the use of prescribed fire on different kinds of vegetation could be listed, but since we will limit our discussion to forest and woodland vegetation, it will suffice to say that on timberland

1. the massive fuel accumulations (burnable debris) that occur where fire is continually excluded are sensibly reduced so that catastrophic wildfires need not happen.

2. the forest develops more diversity in age of trees (young ones do not as often burn up in a cool prescribed burn as in a hot wildfire) and in different kinds of plants (for example, many shrubs are stimulated to sprout more vigorous, new growth).

3. the extreme soil erosion that often follows an all-consuming wildfire—in the long run, likely the greatest cost of wildfire—is avoided in a

prescribed fire, as is the pollution of streams, lakes, and harbors by sediment-laden run-off from devegetated areas.

4. a healthier landscape on which a greater variety of plant life is growing means healthier and more diverse wildlife.

5. many insect and disease problems are decreased, including attacks by tree-killing organisms that plague stagnant, undiversified forestland and cause even more accumulation of fuels.

THE DEPENDENCY OF SOME TYPES OF VEGETATION ON PERIODIC BURNING

Some types of vegetation rely on periodic burning so basically for their well-being that they are really fire-dependent. The *California chaparral* is one example. The *red and white pine forests* of northeastern North America is another. The *piney woods* of the southeastern United States is a third.

Perhaps you hear reports annually in late summer and early autumn of raging wildfire in the mountains of densely settled southern California. These usually occur, or at least start, in the chaparral and are natural to that vegetation type. Of course, fires being intentionally set aggravates the fire hazard of the area, but with or without the activities of man, the chaparral burns periodically. Anyone who builds his home in the midst of chaparral vegetation (and many have) is asking for trouble and loss—and gets it sooner or later.

California chaparral is an impassable brush field, usually standing no more than twice the height of a man. It generally occurs on rugged mountain slopes below five thousand feet elevation where annual precipitation is ten inches or more and summers are dry. Some of the shrubs included in California chaparral are black sage, mountain lilac, scrub oak, manzanita, mountain mahogany, and chamise.

Man can often save himself much difficulty and sorrow by observing nature carefully and adjusting his plans in accordance with his observations. For example, a man may desire to build his home along a stream; but if the stream floods periodically, he should plan to build on higher ground. This is also true for anyone electing to live in the California chaparral. Because of the fire dependency of California chaparral, it is wise to locate elsewhere.

Aside from the fact that by the midtwentieth century southern California had a long-recorded history of periodic fire in the chaparral (Europeans first settled the region in 1769), the natural evidence of the fire-dependent character of chaparral speaks for itself. An observer of the fire-scorched chaparral may notice several things.

First, when an area of chaparral reaches maturity—in one or two generations of mankind—it is not long before it is burned by wildfire. Trees that would come into the chaparral at higher elevations are not able to because they cannot survive the repeated burning that is natural in chaparral. If man suppresses fires in an area so that the chaparral does not burn so frequently, it is only a more ravaging fire when it does.

Second, in the spring following a fire in the chaparral, the wildflower display—and the great benefit it gives as ground cover—is at its densest (and prettiest). This means that these wildflowers depend on fire in the chaparral to clear the way so that they can grow and multiply, and the soil on which they grow relies on their help against erosion. This too shows that God's design for chaparral is repeated burning.

Third, the crowns of the stark, charred scrub

are still very much alive after a fire, and they resprout vigorously.

Fourth, (admittedly this requires closer observation) the seeds of chaparral shrubs have a dormancy designed to be broken by the heat of fire. It is after fire that seedlings of chaparral brush appear.

No one need be taken by surprise that chaparral is destined to burn. God made it a readable page in the Book of Nature, but to their peril, many have ignored what is written there.

The red and white pine forests of southeastern Canada and the northeastern United States depend on fire to keep other forest types from dominating their area. Based on the hardwood invasion that has been occurring in red and white pine forests since Europeans settled in North America, it appears that without fire, pines are replaced in a few centuries by other kinds of trees that are not so tolerant of fire.

Jack pine, a tree associated with red and white pine but growing on the poorest soils in their region, is more directly dependent on fire for its survival than are red and white pines. It needs heat to release the seed from its cones. Forest fires supply this heat, melting the pitch that glues

A mature jack pine

the scales of the cones together. Jack pine cones can persist on the tree unopened for many years.

After a fire, seeds fall from the newly unsealed cones onto the forest floor. The same fire that provided the heat to open the cones of the jack pine also prepares the soil to receive their seed. Bare soil is exposed for a seedbed (not usually a great problem later for soil erosion because jack pines favor open, very sandy soils), competition from other plants is temporarily eliminated, and a flush of nutrients is supplied by the layer of ash left on the ground surface.

Like the red and white pine forests of the Northeast, the pine forests of the southeastern United States are largely replaced by hardwoods unless there is recurring fire. These fires must occur often enough that a situation of *ladder fuels* does not develop.

Fuel ladders occur when there is burnable material all the way from the ground to the crowns of the trees. In such cases grass and low shrubs are fuels that burn to ignite taller shrubs and small trees. Then these intermediate trees and shrubs carry fire into the tops of the tall trees, and an extremely destructive fire results. Such hot crown fires are most common where cooler

The cones of the jack pine need the heat of the forest fires to melt the pitch that glues the scales together so that the seeds can be released.

The twig of a jack pine with unopened cones

burning has not occurred often enough to reduce the burnable materials in the forest understory.

There is a tendency for a fuel ladder to develop especially quickly where many vines grow in the woods. From the viewpoint of fire management, such materials are called *drape*. Drape is a direct connection between ground fuels and treetops. It is important to keep drape under control. Fire is necessary to maintain the pine forests of the Southeast, but it is prescribed in moderation so as to fit the needs of specific areas. Drape complicates fire management. It can suddenly turn a prescribed, controlled fire into a wildfire.

FIRE AND THE SPIRITUAL LIFE

Fire causes chaparral scrub to sprout new, vigorous growth.

It is in the power of the Almighty to turn fiery trials to work for our good. When we rely on His strength, our "faith, being much more precious than of gold that perisheth, though it be tried with fire, [will] be found unto praise and honour and glory at the appearing of Jesus Christ" (1 Peter 1:7). What would seem to cause irreparable damage turns out rather to stimulate desirable and much needed spiritual growth.

LEARNING FROM THE BOOK OF NATURE

The heat of the fire opens jack pine cones to disperse their seed.

Sometimes we need fire from the Lord to open us up to disperse the Gospel. This is how it was for the disciples as they tarried in Jerusalem at Jesus' command, waiting to receive power to preach to all nations. "And when the day of Pentecost was fully come, they were all with one accord in one place. And suddenly there came a sound from heaven as of a rushing mighty wind, and it filled all the house where they were sitting. And there appeared unto them cloven tongues like as of fire, and it sat upon each of them. And they were all filled with the Holy Ghost, and began to speak with other tongues, as the Spirit gave them utterance" (Acts 2:1–4).

In the piney woods of the Southeast, fire has something of a purifying nature.

Fire limits the growth of the hardwoods that so aggressively compete with the pines of the southeastern forests. Fire prescribed at proper intervals controls the height of underbrush and draping vines that become ladder fuels when they grow near to the canopy of the forest. A common southeastern pine, the longleaf pine, dies in the seedling stage from brown spot disease if it does not undergo fire periodically. Fire destroys disease organisms without killing the young pines.

The Scriptures use fire figuratively to indicate the purifying work of God in the lives of men. When the prophet Isaiah saw the Lord, he despaired. "Woe is me! for I am undone; because I am a man of unclean lips, and I dwell in the midst of a people of unclean lips: for mine eyes have seen the King, the Lord of hosts" (Isaiah 6:5).

But the Lord purified Isaiah's lips so that he could speak for Him. "Then flew one of the seraphims unto me, having a live coal in his hand, which he had taken with the tongs from off the altar: and he laid it upon my mouth, and said, Lo, this hath touched thy lips; and thine iniquity is taken away, and thy sin purged" (verses 6, 7).

In one sense Christ's first coming was for the purification of mankind, so that the faithful under the Old Testament might be cleansed and holy, ready to meet Him at His second coming. "But who may abide the day of his coming? and who shall stand when he appeareth? for he is like a refiner's fire, and like fullers' soap: and he shall sit as a refiner and purifier of silver: and he shall purify the sons of Levi, and purge them as gold and silver, that they may offer unto the Lord an offering in righteousness" (Malachi 3:2, 3).

Heaven is a pure and holy place. Sin will never enter there. When Christ returns, He will perform the ultimate purification, "in flaming fire taking vengeance on them that know not God, and that obey not the gospel of our Lord Jesus Christ" (2 Thessalonians 1:8). This is God's counsel for the meantime: "Buy of me gold tried in the fire, that thou mayest be rich" (Revelation 3:18).

Then, "when he hath tried me, I shall come forth as gold" (Job 23:10).

"Beloved, think it not strange concerning the fiery trial which is to try you, as though some strange thing happened unto you:

"But rejoice, inasmuch as ye are partakers of Christ's sufferings; that, when his glory shall be revealed, ye may be glad also with exceeding joy.

"If ye be reproached for the name of Christ, happy are ye."

1 Peter 4:12–14

Chapter 8

WEEDS

Thorns and Thistles

What is the final answer to weeds?

A friend tells how as a Kansas farm boy he dreaded above all other chores the grubbing out of thistles from the pastures and fields. Once as his family was laboring together at this task, he confessed his feelings to his grandfather. The wise old man paused in his efforts, straightened his back for a moment, and silently contemplated the great sweep of the plains. "Willy," he said at last, "when I see these thistles, it reminds me that God's Word is true."

In Genesis 3 one of God's first promises to fallen man is a curse on the earth: "Thorns also and thistles shall it bring forth to thee." This marks the beginning of man's struggle with weeds.

The literal fulfillment of this aspect of God's judgment is much in evidence today. In the mid-1960s crop losses and costs due to weed control in the United States alone were estimated at over five billion dollars a year. Effects of weeds on man include much more than undernourished, out-competed crops and the resulting reduced yields. Quality of grain and dairy products is impaired by wild onions, wild garlic, and ragweed in forage. There are weeds that injure livestock or make them sick, and there are those that poison people when their seeds are present in food. Others are capable of causing allergic reactions merely through contact with the skin.

Green plant parts from weeds harvested along with grain can contribute to spoilage. Hay is made less palatable to livestock by the presence of some kinds of weeds. Valuable irrigation water is consumed by weeds lining ditch banks, and at the other extreme, drainage ditches may be clogged by water weeds. Certain weeds are hosts to insects and diseases that attack crop plants. Even crop plants themselves, such as the Johnson grass and kudzu of the southeastern United States, can become of greater significance as weeds than they are as crops.

Finally, land values are diminished by weed infestations, and the work of a giant combine during corn harvest in the Great Lakes states can be made ineffective by a dense growth of lowly quack grass.

If we take "thorns and thistles" as an environmental type and include insect and disease losses and control along with weeds, we can enlarge annual costs of American crop losses in the mid-1960s to over thirteen billion dollars. Other "weeds" in our environment could include drought, floods, frost, heat waves, hail, urban encroachment on farmland, and soil erosion.

Some of man's devices to control his environment are often worse than the "weeds" themselves. For example, fortunes are spent on control of weeds, insects, and disease, and our environment is further degraded by some of the methods used. Productive land is inverted or destroyed by surface mining. Irrigation waters may become too salty to use. Air is polluted by emissions from refineries, factories, and motor vehicles.

The world today is very different from the

Garden of Eden that God gave to Adam. Indeed, it differs even from the world of Noah's time, and more recently yet, from the less degraded environment so beautifully described in Psalm 104.

A third way of viewing "thorns and thistles" is in a figurative sense. They are symbols of sickness, both spiritually and physically. The Bible tells us what will happen if we do not faithfully "weed" our spiritual gardens. Weeds of the cares of this life and the love of material things will choke out the Word in our lives. "And the care of this world, and the deceitfulness of riches, choke the word, and he becometh unfruitful" (Matthew 13:7, 22).

Such weeds grow in the lives of those who would lead men away from God, and we can tell false prophets by the weeds in their lives. "Wherefore by their fruits ye shall know them" (Matthew 7:15-20). Romans 1:18-32 expounds the spiritual degeneration that results from uncontrolled weediness in our personal lives. "Because that, when they knew God, they glorified him not as God, neither were thankful; but became vain in their imaginations, and their foolish heart was darkened" (verse 21). Read particularly Romans 1:28-32 for the names of the vicious weeds that consume the lives of the ungodly.

Before His crucifixion, we see the Saviour of mankind mockingly crowned with thorns, the bitter symbol of man's earthly travail and the rightful symbol of God's judgment upon man's sin.

Yet it was not the crown of thorns and the Crucifixion that had the final word. The empty tomb is God's positive answer to man's greatest question: "Is there life after death?" The empty tomb is God's way of drawing our gaze beyond the certainty of death and decay demonstrated in natural ecology. Through the resurrected Christ, we can look to a perfect, eternal land watered by the pure river of the water of life, where "there shall be no more curse" (Revelation 22:1–3).

Chapter 9

WOODPECKERS

Red-Head and Scarlet-Crest

God has well-equipped the woodpeckers for their natural work—how will He equip us for the spiritual work He has for us?

RED-HEAD

Red-head flew from her nest hole in the top of a dead elm snag. Scarlet head, white chest, and white midwings were vivid against glossy black. In a graceful, swinging arc she flew a short distance to a sunny hillside. Landing, she tore into a large anthill and began licking up the ants that excitedly emerged to investigate the disturbance.

Back at the skeletal elm, in her nest cavity forty feet above ground, were five baby red-headed woodpeckers. They were almost four weeks old. In the next day or two they would be leaving the nest. As yet, Red-head and her mate were continually busy locating food to satisfy their hearty, noisily voiced appetites.

Each day the parents gathered wild berries and seeds, raided the orchard at the nearby farm, and captured insects and spiders to feed their young and themselves. Occasionally one of them would catch a mouse, feed at a nest of bird's eggs, or kill a small young bird. Because of the wide variety in their diet and their ability to obtain food on the ground, on shrubs and trees, and in the air, they were able to obtain food easily. (Nor should we forget their famous ability to bore insects out of trees, logs, stumps, and utility poles.)

When their first hatch of baby woodpeckers had been in the nest cavity two-and-one-half months earlier, food had been even easier to get. Then the parents had preyed heavily on the abundant population of May beetles (or June bugs).

Before Red-head had laid that first clutch of six snow-white eggs, the nest cavity had been excavated sixteen inches deep, with an entrance hole two inches wide. It was hollowed out to about four inches in diameter, and the bottom was covered with a layer of fine chips rapped off the walls. The sides of the nest cavity were finished off smoothly.

Before the second clutch of eggs was laid in midsummer, a fresh layer of wood chips was chiseled off the walls and left as a layer a few inches thick over the old nest. Fourteen days after Red-head laid the first egg, the second set of baby woodpeckers began to hatch out on the clean bedding. The parents had taken turns at incubating the eggs, and at night one had remained on the nest while the other stayed in another hole in the same tree.

Prior to carrying coarse food to their young, Red-head and her mate took time to prepare it. They used an oak stump near their elm snag as a table and cutting board. There they butchered and processed their provisions, saving only digestible parts for their young.

By the time the young woodpeckers were old enough to leave the nest, they wore their immature plumage. Having dull-black backs with spotted, streaked, grayish-brown feathers

Red-headed woodpecker on a dead elm snag

elsewhere on their bodies, they did not look much like their parents. Their wings resembled their father's and mother's but were not as showy in their contrasts of black and white. However, in early autumn they would begin to molt. Before mating season next year, they would have most of their adult plumage.

When Red-head's first nest of offspring of this season had left the nest hole, they were sufficiently mature to provide for themselves, but at first she and her mate had continued to bring food to them irregularly. This did not last long. Before the second group of eggs had been hatched, their parents had driven the fledglings out of the area.

Another cycle of parental care had begun.

*   *   *   *   *

Around Red-head's home in northern Indiana it has turned out to be a good year for wild crops. Beechnuts and acorns are abundant, so Red-head and her mate do not join in the fall migration southward. Here, as autumn advances into winter, they will be willing to share territory with other red headed woodpeckers. And, while this is of no concern to them, it is interesting for us to conjecture that they may be reunited with their offspring as they live and play in the wintry woods.

SCARLET-CREST

Inside her nest cavity at a barkless old beech standing by a riverbank in the forests of central Pennsylvania, Scarlet-crest sensed that her mate would soon be relieving her. It had been almost two hours since she had begun her turn at incubating their clutch of four glossy white eggs.

The pair of pileated woodpeckers had used the same snag as a nesting tree for four years, each year excavating a new cavity at a different height between twenty-five and fifty feet above the ground on its south or east side. This year mice began residing in their second year's hole at twenty-five feet, and last year a wood duck had used their oldest, highest hole to hatch and raise her brood.

When the mice and the wood duck hen had discovered their accommodations, they each had found a hole lacking any trace of previous habitations except, perhaps, for a fluffy feather or two. The woodpeckers had kept their nest spotlessly clean, carrying away all wastes.

In April of this year Scarlet-crest had used her mighty bill to begin excavating and shaping the nest cavity while her mate occupied himself elsewhere in the area. After chipping out an entrance hole three-and-one-half inches across, she had dug out a cavity nineteen inches deep, tapering it from eight inches near the top down to a bowl-shaped bottom six inches wide. After the inside of the hole had been finished, the only nesting materials left to cushion the eggs were small splinters of wood. Walls of dry, solid beech four inches thick would protect their young.

Soon, as she had anticipated, her mate approached the snag, landing first in the branches of a nearby sugar maple and then flying to the snag. Large, clawed toes and a stiff, bracing tail assured him of a good hold on the smooth stub as he waited to switch places in the nest cavity.

As Scarlet-crest perched on the beveled edge of the nest's entrance hole, they exchanged soft calls. Only an experienced observer could have told male from female. Both of these crow-sized birds were dull black with sharply contrasting, narrow white stripes on their faces, extending down onto their shoulders. Each had a striking red crest. The only notable differences were the greater extent of red feathering of the male's crest—onto his forehead—and the possession of a red cheek patch by him only. As Scarlet-crest flew away from the dead snag, conspicuous white patches at midwing and on wing tips flashed against the green canopy of the forest.

Gracefully gliding and slowly flapping her way through the predominantly hardwood forest, Scarlet-crest flew to an old, dying hemlock and began stripping off large chunks of bark. She was searching for her favorite source of food—a colony of ants. On the warm days ahead, she and her mate would work at this and similar trees, seeking ants, beetles, and other insects. Also, they would tear into rotting stumps and logs, overturn layers of moss, and disrupt anthills. As wild fruits and nuts matured, they would feed on dogwood and holly berries, cherries, beechnuts, acorns, and others.

It is in freezing weather, however, that they will begin the work that is a telltale sign of the residence of pileated woodpeckers in a forest. Resoundingly hammering away with their specially designed beaks, they will make impressive scars on dead and living trees as they excavate pits and troughs into heartwood, reaching overwintering colonies of ants. Using spearlike tongues, they will extract insects from deep in the recesses of the colonies. They will make no mistakes in selection; they will always attack only weakened, infested trees. Boring and chipping off splinters up to three inches long and one inch wide, they will make rectangular trenches up to eight inches wide, a foot or more long, and as deep as the heartwood. Where one trench joins another, a long furrow down the trunk will result. If the shape of the colony is square, then square pits will be dug.

 After feeding heavily on ants, Scarlet-crest returned to the nest hole to relieve her mate. They had ten more days to go in their eighteen-day incubation period.

 In the first days after hatching their young, the parents will relieve one another more often than before, but each will remain in the nest cavity until the other returns from food collecting. As the baby birds grow, constant attention will cease, and feeding will be done at approximately one-half hour intervals, mostly by Scarlet-crest. While the adult birds will stay largely silent around the nest snag, the young birds, when they sense the arrival of their parents with food, will stretch forth their necks and screech. (Pileated woodpeckers feed their young by regurgitating partly digested food from their own stomachs into their offsprings' mouths.)

As always, Scarlet-crest and her mate will raise only one brood this year. Their clutch of eggs will hatch in mid-May, and the young birds will leave the nest in mid-June. After leaving the nest they will remain with their parents for some time, at first receiving food from them. As they grow, they will begin searching for wild fruits and the more easily accessible types of insects. Later, as their bills harden, they too will bore and excavate for food.

Scarlet-crest, her mate, and their offspring are year-round residents of their Pennsylvania woods. When other birds depart for warmer areas, they and their kind stay behind. They find shelter on winter nights and wait out freezing winter storms in their snug, dry holes, high above the snowy forest floor.

FULLY EQUIPPED

The woodpeckers have been wonderfully designed by God for the accomplishment of their work. They are provided with bodies fully equipped for their specialization as woodborers. Not only do they obtain a large part of their food by drilling into and tearing away at trees, stumps, and logs, but also they excavate holes for nest cavities for their young and, for some kinds of woodpeckers, as shelter for themselves.

Behind a strong, chisel-like bill, the woodpecker has a large, sturdy skull set on a powerfully muscled neck. On the bill the nostrils are covered by tiny brush feathers that keep out wood dust and chips.

Inside the bill is an especially long, thin, and flexible tongue. For these wood-boring insect feeders the tongue has a hard, spear-shaped tip and is rimmed with bristles. Glands at the base of the tongue are well situated to coat it with a sticky mucus to assist in catching insect prey.

Not only are these interesting birds masterfully provided with tools to excavate holes and capture insects, they also have the legs, feet, and tail needed to stay at their work. (Young woodpeckers leave the nest cavity and climb on the tree before they fly.) Legs are relatively short, and feet are strong. There are four toes—two that reach forward and two behind—with large, curved claws to grip the tree. A stiff, strongly shafted tail braces the bird from below.

God has fully equipped the woodpecker for its functions. It goes without saying that except for His all-providing, masterful hand, such interesting, hardworking birds as these could not possibly fulfill their role in nature.

God has assigned tasks to Christians that are impossible for ordinary men and women to accomplish. However, it is Christ that makes *ordinary* men and women *extraordinary*: "For without me ye can do nothing" (John 15:5).

When the Lord calls us to His work, He provides the equipment to accomplish the task, the instructions for its use, and, for our assurance and edification, the reasons that we need it.

"Put on the whole armour of God, that ye may be able to stand against the wiles of the devil. For we wrestle not against flesh and blood, but against principalities, against powers, against the rulers of the darkness of this world, against spiritual wickedness in high places. Wherefore take unto you the whole armour of God, that ye may be able to withstand in the evil day, and having done all, to stand. Stand therefore, having your loins girt about with truth, and having on the breastplate of righteousness; and your feet shod with the preparation of the gospel of peace; above all, taking the shield of faith, wherewith ye shall be able to quench all the fiery darts of the wicked. And take the helmet of salvation, and the sword of the Spirit, which is the Word of God: praying always with all prayer and supplication in the Spirit, and watching thereunto with all perseverance and supplication for all saints; and for me, that utterance may be given unto me, that I may open my mouth boldly, to make known the mystery of the gospel" (Ephesians 6:11–19).

The whole armor of God: truth, righteousness, the Gospel of peace, faith, salvation, and the Word of God—this is the equipment that alone will protect laborers of Christ against the wiles of the devil. However, as we boldly witness to the power of the Gospel, we must also remember prayer. As the pileated woodpecker seeks its hole to regain strength to meet a new day and find refuge through the night, so do we Christians need prayer in the secret closet, a place of rest wherein God revives and strengthens us to remain at the work.

Chapter 10

ANIMALS AND TOOLS

Not Hammers and Saws, But Tools Nonetheless

What do you think is the most important tool?

Some animals have the ability to use tools. For these creatures, using tools is not just an occasional happening. It is their ordinary way of doing things. In many cases it is necessary for their survival. God gave these animals their tool-using abilities, and He provides the tools they need.

Some tool-using creatures might seem to us to be quite "feeble folk," such as spiders and insects. For example:

• The *bolas spider* makes only a single line of silk,

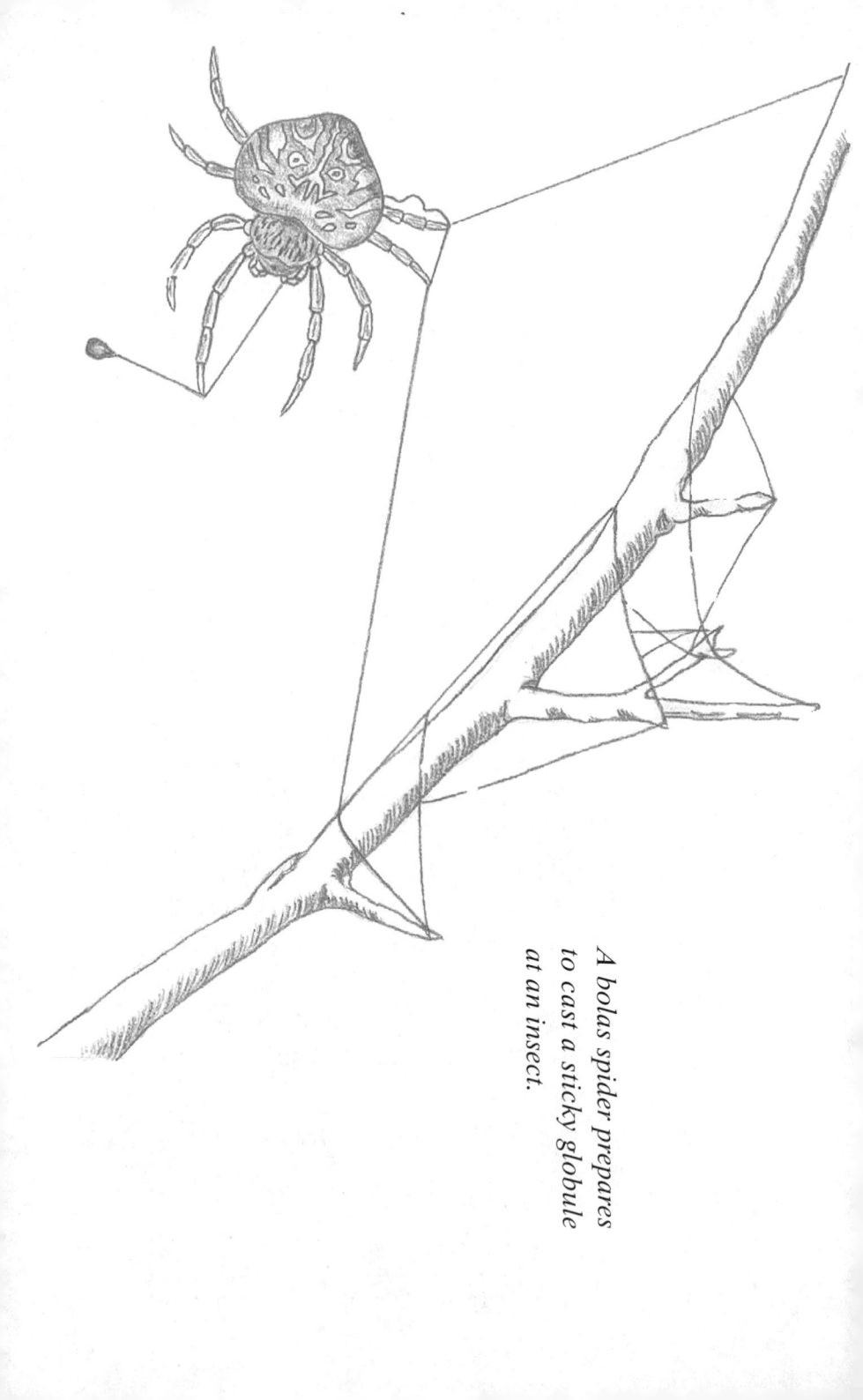

A bolas spider prepares to cast a sticky globule at an insect.

but this solitary line has a sticky globule at its end. The spider swings the line at its insect prey, which is caught on the sticky ball.
- The *thread-waisted wasp* uses a pebble as a hammer. When it seals the entrance to its nest burrow, the wasp holds the pebble in its mandibles and pounds on the soil covering the entry, compacting it for the protection of its young and their food supply.
- Adult *weaver ants* use the silk-making ability of their larvae to bind together the materials for their leaf nests. An ant carries a larva in its mandibles, pressing the larva's mouth against the surfaces it wishes to bind together. The larva releases its silk-forming secretions on the surface of the leaf or branch; then the ant moves it to another point. Repeated movement of the larva from point to point by the adult results in a woven leaf nest. In this case the animal's tool is not only another living creature—the tool is one of the animal's own kind.

The use of tools is not limited to animals on land.
- A hungry little *archer fish* spits a four-foot jet of water to skillfully knock an insect off an

LEARNING FROM THE BOOK OF NATURE

overhanging plant into its pool.
- A *hermit crab* places a sea anemone on its shell house for partial protection from enemies.

Also, God created some birds to be tool users.
- The *Galapagos woodpecker finch* holds a cactus spine in its beak and probes the wood of a decaying tree for insects.
- An *Egyptian vulture* feeds on an ostrich egg it broke open by throwing a stone with its beak.
- *Weaverbirds* weave and knot blades of grass around forked twigs of trees to make sturdy basket-like nests. One kind, the *red-headed weaverbird,* builds with twigs knotted together by bark it has peeled back from the twigs.
- The *tailorbird* of southern Asia chooses a large, living leaf and sews its edges together to make an envelope to hold its nest. Its bill serves as its needle, and plant fibers are its thread.

The Lord created tool users among the beasts, small and great.
- *Elephants* use their trunks to grasp sticks to scratch themselves. At other times their trunks grip branches to swing at tormenting insects otherwise out of reach.

Animals and Tools

- Locating a tree loaded with ripened nuts, a troop of *brown capuchin monkeys* uses stones to hammer the nuts open.
- Two *beavers* discover a hole in their dam. One fetches a stone and holds it over the hole while the other plasters it in place with mud.
- To prevent drifting with the currents, a *sea otter* wraps itself in kelp before beginning its floating nap.
- Grasping a rock between its forepaws, a *polar bear* smashes through the ice to get a seal.
- The wild *chimpanzee* does not face the novel situations man arranges for tame ones; but his innate capabilities are the work of God, so he is already an accomplished tool user in his natural environment.

In rain chimpanzees use large leaves as umbrellas.

Chimpanzees have various uses for sticks. Termites cling to the stick a chimpanzee thrusts into their mound; then the chimpanzec withdraws the stick and eats the termites. Sticks are wedged into cracks and crevices and then used as steps. Also, chimpanzees use sticks to gather in or knock down objects that are out of reach.

THE MOST IMPORTANT TOOL

The Creator provides the needed tools and endows His creatures with the ability to use them. Let this draw our minds to His spiritual provision for mankind.

We do not think we are selfish in saying that the Bible is very useful. God gave it to us, and He intends that we use it. As His Word, it can and should be our chief and best tool in life. Indeed, if it is not the tool we rely on above all others, we are sure to be faulty workmen.

The Bible is a multipurpose, all-sufficient tool. The truths in the pages of God's Word start us on the Christian way. They guide us along the Christian path. They never wear out.

We use the Bible for *encouragement.*

"Thy words were found, and I did eat them; and thy word was unto me the joy and rejoicing of mine heart: for I am called by thy name, O Lord God of hosts" (Jeremiah 15:16).

In it we find *wise counsel.*

"O that my ways were directed to keep thy statutes! Then shall I not be ashamed, when I have respect unto all thy commandments" (Psalm 109:5, 6).

Animals and Tools

We rely on the Bible to help move us in true *worship*—to lift our thoughts higher than ourselves, to draw our minds to God.

"O send out thy light and thy truth: let them lead me; let them bring me unto thy holy hill, and to thy tabernacles" (Psalm 43:3).

Really, we might question whether this tool God gave us is being used by *us*, or by *God* on our behalf. We read in Ephesians 6 that it is the sword of His Spirit. It is superior to any cutting instrument man can devise.

"For the word of God is quick, and powerful, and sharper than any twoedged sword, piercing even to the dividing asunder of soul and spirit, and of the joints and marrow, and is a discerner of the thoughts and intents of the heart" (Hebrews 4:12).

Also, the Holy Scriptures are "like a hammer that breaketh the rock in pieces" (Jeremiah 23:29). The greatest thing that happens to anyone occurs when the hardened heart is broken by this hammer, the Word of God. Then God gives a new heart, now tender with the love of Jesus—a new heart yearning for its eternal home.

What a treasure God gave us in the Bible: O wonderful, wonderful, *useful* Word!

O Wonderful, Wonderful Word

O wonderful, wonderful Word of the Lord!
    True wisdom its pages unfold;
And though we may read them a thousand times o'er,
    They never, no never grow old!
Each line hath a treasure, each promise a pearl,
    That all, if they will, may secure;
And we know that when time and the world pass away,
    God's Word shall forever endure.

O wonderful, wonderful Word of the Lord!
    The lamp that our Father above
So kindly has lighted to teach us the way
    That leads to the arms of His love!
Its warnings, its counsels, are faithful and just;
    Its judgments are perfect and pure;
And we know that when time and the world pass away,
    God's Word shall forever endure.

Animals and Tools

O wonderful, wonderful Word of the Lord!
    Our only salvation is there;
It carries conviction down deep in the heart,
    And shows us ourselves as we are.
It tells of a Saviour, and points to the cross,
    Where pardon we now may secure,
For we know that when time and the world pass away,
    God's Word shall forever endure.

O wonderful, wonderful Word of the Lord!
    The hope of our friends in the past;
Its truth, where so firmly they anchored their trust,
    Through ages eternal shall last.
O wonderful, wonderful Word of the Lord!
    Unchanging, abiding, and sure;
For we know that when time and the world pass away,
    God's Word shall forever endure.

                                  —Fanny J. Crosby

Chapter 11

WATERSHEDS

The Continental Divide

When can a watershed work backwards?

I first heard of the Continental Divide when I was a schoolboy. Our teacher told us that rainfall on one side of this line joins waters flowing into the Pacific Ocean, but rainfall on the other side ultimately drains into the Atlantic Ocean.

This explanation sparked my imagination. I envisioned lofty peaks and towering crags along the backbone of North America, where precipitation was divided and destined for one or the other of the great oceans. (Imagine my sense of irony when twenty years later I crossed the Continental Divide in west central New Mexico on the low rises of a dusty plain covered with grass and rabbitbrush.)

Closely related to the concept of continental divide is the concept of *watersheds*. Each stream has its watershed. That watershed includes all the land that drains water into the stream.

Each watershed has a natural boundary (or divide) that separates it and its runoff from other watersheds around it. Thus, the land astride the Great Divide of our continent can be thought of in terms of the groups of watersheds draining into either the Pacific Ocean (such as the Colorado and Columbia River watersheds), Atlantic Ocean (such as the Mississippi and St. Lawrence River watersheds), or Arctic Ocean (for example, the Mackenzie River watershed).

As you think about watersheds and divides, you can easily see that large watersheds are made up of smaller ones. The Mississippi River watershed includes the smaller watersheds of several other large rivers and streams, such as the Arkansas, Missouri, and Ohio rivers. These, in turn, receive runoff from yet smaller rivers. This system of smaller tributary watersheds continues right up into our local creeks and seasonally dry drainage ways.

Watersheds

The rule is this: the water flowing in any stream has drained off that stream's *watershed*—the area of land surrounding the stream that is separated from the watersheds of other streams by a divide.

The watershed is a very useful concept. Engineers must know the size, climate, and land characteristics of a watershed to properly design a dam on a river for hydroelectric power or water storage. A farmer must plan similarly as he lays out field terraces and farm ponds. A home buyer should investigate these matters if he considers buying a house near a stream channel. Errors in understanding or in judgment on this point have often resulted in great expense and inconvenience, and sometimes in disaster and heartbreak.

As mentioned, some watersheds are great—such as the 2 1/2 million square miles of the Amazon River watershed in South America. However, the half acre in Farmer Martin's pasture at the head of the dry fork of Little Creek may also be a watershed. Watersheds are rough and steep, such as in mountainous regions, or smooth and flat, as on coastal plains. They can be as arid as the Arabian wadi or as saturated as the Congo.

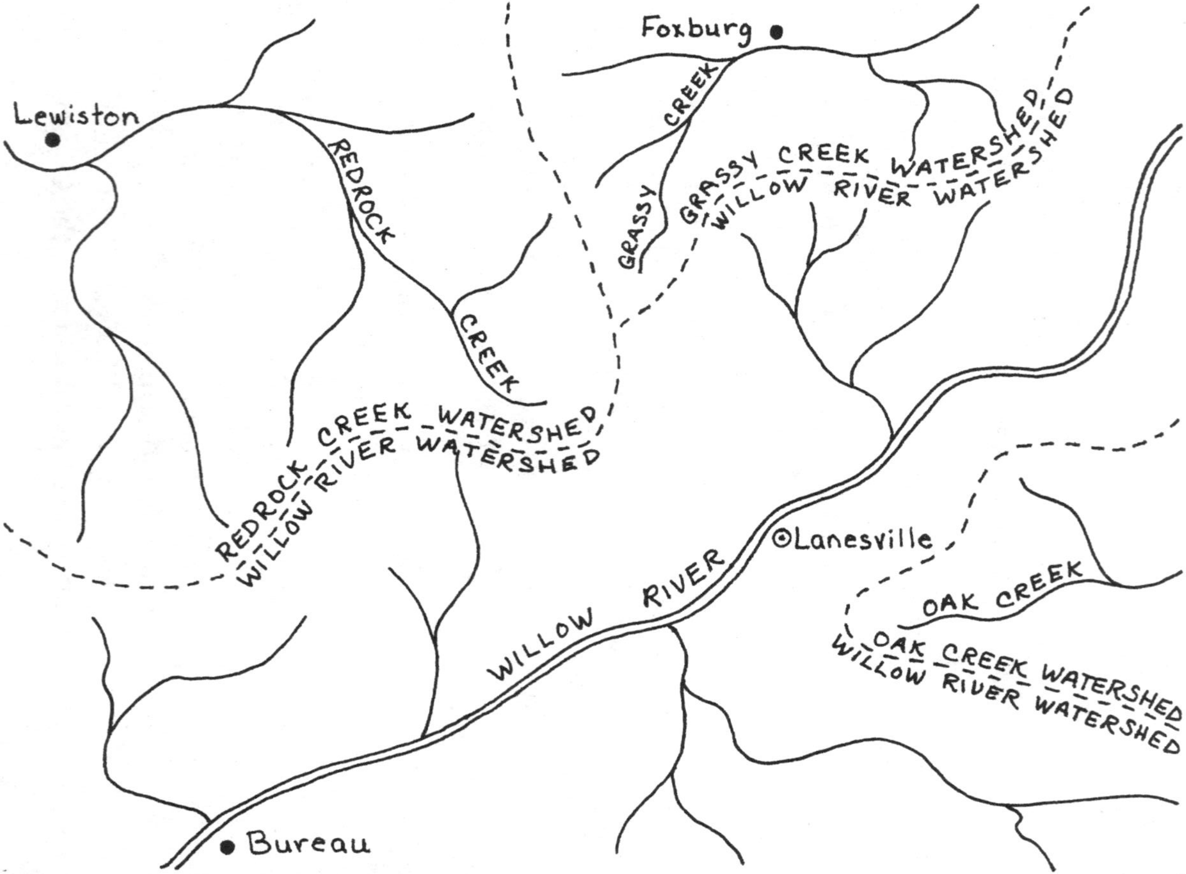
Foxburg
Lewiston
GRASSY CREEK
REDROCK
CREEK
GRASSY CREEK WATERSHED
WILLOW RIVER WATERSHED
REDROCK CREEK WATERSHED
WILLOW RIVER WATERSHED
Lanesville
WILLOW RIVER
OAK CREEK
OAK CREEK WATERSHED
WILLOW RIVER WATERSHED
Bureau

Watersheds

For the moment, let us look at our lives as watersheds. Many claim that wherever we are at a given time in our thinking, our work, and our social life, we are there as a result of influences on us and the decisions that we have made in relation to them. As with water in a natural watershed, these influences and decisions have channeled into our lives so that at any point in time we are what we are, and we think what we think, largely because of them. Thus we exist from day to day merely enlarging our life's watershed as we go, controlled and conditioned by our experiences.

According to this line of thinking, our actions are really reactions, and as with the water in a stream, we become the expression of what the world we have passed through has done to us.

This line of thought often seems to be true for the natural man. But, praise God, He has

Caption for facing page:
Several streams and the natural divides between them. Redrock, Grassy, and Oak Creeks are all tributaries to rivers other than Willow River—otherwise they would be included in the Willow River watershed.

made a way out of it! It is a way that opens up suddenly when we agree with God, confess that we have sinned, repent with godly sorrow, and are justified and made new creatures before Him through the death and resurrection of Jesus Christ. "Behold, now is the accepted time; behold, now is the day of salvation" (2 Corinthians 6:2).

Starting at this point, the watershed of life begins working in reverse. Life without God was merely one of reacting to the flow of daily experiences on the basis of past influences. In this new life, our way of being and doing starts with Jesus Christ and continues in the power of His Holy Spirit. Rather than everything funneling into us and controlling us, God's love, life, and control fan out of us into all areas of our lives. We are no longer the affected-by-the-world but the effective-for-Christ.

This, of course, seems a very *unnatural* way of living. Does it seem unlikely that rivers will flow in reverse, carrying their water back into the uplands? Unless he is saved through Jesus Christ, how much more impossible it is for man to begin to live free of the mortal watershed. If we are to rise and remain out of the channels of the sinful society about us, we must begin and continue a daily walk with God. Then we will be spiritual *water sources.*

"He that believeth on me, as the scripture hath said, out of his belly shall flow rivers of living water" (John 7:38).

Chapter 12

CAMOUFLAGE AND MIMICRY

Pretense

Can camouflage and mimicry be Christian virtues?

Using simple devices under cover of night to imitate a large army, Gideon and three hundred men set the great host of Midian in panic. . . . At Gath, David mimicked a madman. . . . Secretly following Jesus to the palace of the high priest, Peter attempted to hide his identity as one of Jesus' disciples by blending with the crowd.

Often we see people pretending to be what they are not. Others try to fit into the crowd without being noticed. If it does not occur independently to man to hide or deceive by social

LEARNING FROM THE BOOK OF NATURE

camouflage and mimicry, the idea could come from nature. For example:

- During its nighttime foraging, a *Malayan tapir* is effectively camouflaged from its predators by the white belt around its middle. Though contrasting to its black forequarters and hindquarters in daytime, at night this white belt breaks up the tapir's outline among the shadowy, moonlit vegetation.
- The *sphinx moth* is patterned to match the tree bark it rests on; but when it is disturbed, a sudden flash of its brightly colored underwings startles its enemies.
- The *living stone cactus,* really a succulent, escapes the notice of foraging animals because it looks so much like the surrounding gravel.

These are three examples of *camouflage*—the similarity in appearance between a plant or animal and its surroundings that allows it to escape the notice of its predators.

Camouflage and mimicry are very common phenomena in nature. *Mimicry*, in the natural sense, is a close resemblance between an animal and a plant (or even a part of a plant) or between one kind of animal and a different kind of animal.

Camouflage: a moth, the great oak beauty with its newly laid eggs, spreads its wings so that it blends with its background—the bark of a tree.

For instance:
- A *bee hawk moth* has a similar appearance to a bumblebee, so bumblebees stay out of its feeding area.
- *Treehoppers* are juicy, plant-sucking insects, but insect-eating birds are fooled by their resemblance to thorns; the younger stage of the adult treehopper, the nymph, looks like a rough spot on the bark. (See picture on page 131.)
- *Flower mantises* look like attractive pink or white flowers. The flower mantis demonstrates dual reliance on mimicry: it is able to merely lie in wait for its insect prey to come to it, while being virtually invisible to the eyes of birds that would prey on it.

Even with the definitions given earlier for *camouflage* and *mimicry,* these two methods are a little difficult to keep distinct from one another. In a sense, the hawk moth that mimics the bumblebee is camouflaging its true identity from the bumblebees.

The same is true of the *walking sticks* and the *looper caterpillars*, whose true identities are camouflaged by their mimicry of twigs and sticks, and also of the *viceroy butterfly* that mimics the distasteful (to birds) *monarch butterfly,* whose larva

Mimicry of an insect by another insect: a bee hawk moth looks like a bumblebee.

subsists on milkweed.

However, if we use *camouflage* to mean similarity in appearance to the plant or animal's background, and reserve *mimicry* for when an animal closely resembles a plant or other kind of animal in its environment, the distinction between the two terms should be clear enough.

Camouflage is not used only by relatively defenseless creatures as an aid to survival. As with mimicry, for some predatory animals camouflage is an important part of their hunting strategy. For example:

The stripes on the *tiger's* coat and the plain tawniness of the *lion's* coat appear quite contrasting in a zoo, but both the tiger's stripes and the lion's plainness are a helpful camouflage against the differing backgrounds of their native environments.

A bird of Central and South America, the *potoo* has feathering that matches the patterns of old, rotting tree limbs. The potoo's behavior complements its camouflage. It perches at the end of a tree stub or on top of a fence post, carefully positioning its body so as to appear continuous with the perch, even orienting its beak in line with it.

The *chameleon* is a type of lizard that has the remarkable ability of rapidly changing its color to match its immediate background: green on green leaves, brown on brown leaves and tree bark, or any variation of color between. Camouflage benefits the chameleon, as it does many

Camouflage and Mimicry

other animals, as both predator and prey.

The chameleon is not the only animal to which the Lord gave this ability to change color. For instance:

There are other types of lizards and also frogs, fish, and squid that rely on their color-changing ability for camouflage. Some change color quickly like the chameleon. Others, such as the *crab spider*, change more slowly.

The *crab spider* can change from white to yellow or yellow to white, but several days are required to make the change. It hides in flower blossoms in wait for insects that come to feed on their nectar. In white flowers it will be white, and in yellow flowers it will turn yellow. Such a slow change complements the spider's life, which is attuned to the seasons. Under ordinary conditions, a crab spider will need to change color only gradually, as one kind of flower withers and another kind blooms.

The master of color change among all of God's creatures is the *octopus*. Animals change color by varying the concentration and movement of pigment in color cells. When color pigment spreads out over the cell, the entire cell becomes darker; when a cell's pigment reconcentrates, the cell becomes lighter. An octopus has millions of color cells, termed *chromatophores*. To change color, an octopus expands or contracts these cells: on expansion, color pigment spreads out; on contraction, it reconcentrates.

The octopus has two other types of cells that affect its color. One type, the *iridophore*, reflects light. With the iridophores the octopus can reflect light at the same intensity as its surroundings, greatly reducing its visibility.

The third type of cell affecting the octopus's color is the *leucophore*, which reflects white light. Through changes in its leucophores, the octopus can make itself very pale.

For any animal, camouflage is a shop with more than one tool. The octopus changes not only the color of its skin but also the texture, which may be changed from smooth to rough and warty. This enables it to match the texture of the barnacle-encrusted stones and coral on the sea floor.

The *Indian leaf bug* not only looks like a leaf; it also waves back and forth in imitation of a leaf in the wind.

Many well-camouflaged creatures would be seen if they moved, so they are primarily

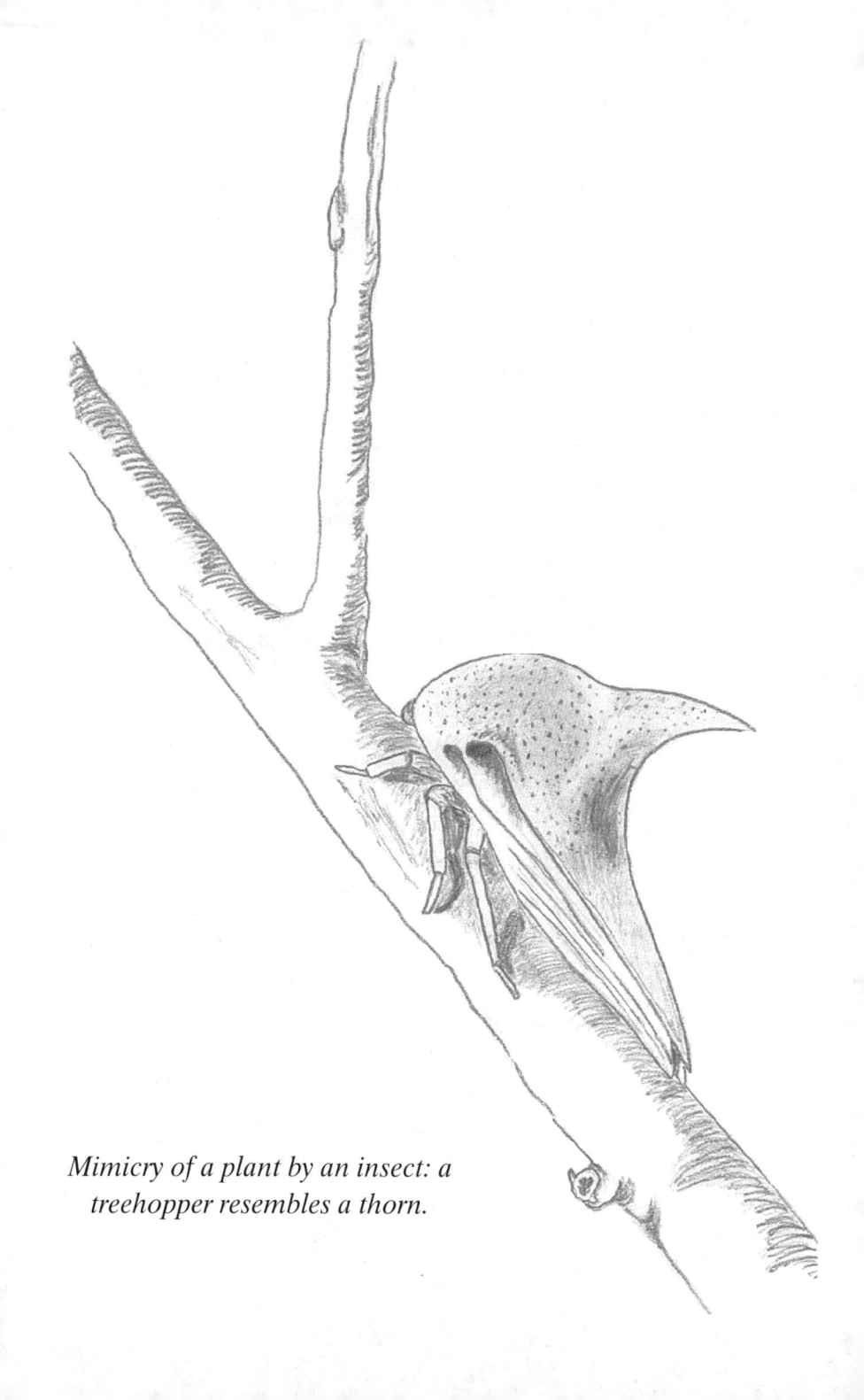

Mimicry of a plant by an insect: a treehopper resembles a thorn.

nocturnal. The *nightjars* of Europe and the aforementioned potoos of Central and South America are two well-camouflaged birds that demonstrate a preference for nocturnal activity.

It is interesting to consider camouflage from a regional viewpoint. For instance, Arctic animals rely on techniques of camouflage that are consistent with their frigid environment: the coats of the *Arctic fox* and the *weasel* turn white in winter so they are not easily detected by prey; the plumage of the *willow ptarmigan* and the coat of the *snowshoe hare* turn white so they are not easily seen by predators.

Desert animals that are camouflaged are concealed in harmony with their arid environment. The *kit fox's* light-colored coat makes it inconspicuous as it stalks a kangaroo rat on a moonlit desert night. The *horned lizard*, another animal able to change its color, takes on the hue of the ground where it lives. It even darkens its scaly skin when in shade and lightens it in sunshine.

Birds that hunt over the sea typically have white feathering underneath, reducing the distinctiveness of their outline against the sky. The *penguin,* a bird that "flies" in the sea, also has

Camouflage and Mimicry

light feathering below. Its light-below, dark-above coloration is like that of most fish; the effect is to make the animal more difficult to observe both from below (looking toward the brighter light of the water's surface) and from above (looking into the darkness of its depths).

The Sargasso Sea is not really a sea in the usual sense. It is a vast, still area of warm water in the middle of the Atlantic Ocean. Seaweed called *sargassum* dominates surface waters in this area. Sargassum is olive brown in color and has small air bladders on its stems that help keep it afloat.

Thoroughgoing camouflage is typical of the animals that inhabit the great rafts of sargassum. The permanent residents of the sargassum are shaped and colored like this seaweed. The *sargassum pipefish* resembles the fronds of sargassum; it is twenty-five times as long as it is thick. The sargassum fish employs both mimicry and camouflage to the extent that it is hard to distinguish it from the seaweed. It is camouflaged by both the texture and color of its skin, and by various knobs and irregularities protruding from its body that mimic the parts of sargassum. It is so masterfully disguised by its camouflage (or is it its mimicry?) that it even possesses white spots that match the tube worms that live on the sargassum.

MAN, MIMICRY, AND CAMOUFLAGE

The Old Testament records several instances of man's humble efforts at camouflage and mimicry that were granted God's apparent blessing. Why is it, then, that New Testament saints did not (and do not) use camouflage and mimicry to gain their ends?

First, they do not need to. Second, God does not want them to. Third, they have no desire to.

The Christian does not need to use camouflage and mimicry because the Spirit of God has come upon him and the enemy can always be met head-on. The risen Christ declared, "Ye shall receive power, after that the Holy Ghost is come upon you" (Acts 1:8). "God hath not given us the spirit of fear; but of power, and of love, and of a sound mind" (2 Timothy 1:7), "so that we may boldly say, The Lord is my helper, and I will not fear what man shall do unto me" (Hebrews 13:6).

As Christians, we need never give place to Satan, for we can put on the whole armor of God so that we may be able to stand against Satan's wiles (Ephesians 6:11). Indeed, "resist the devil, and he will flee from you" (James 4:7).

The New Testament indicates that Christ does not want His followers to use disguise and pretense. "Ye are the light of the world. A city that is set on an hill cannot be hid. Neither do men light a candle, and put it under a bushel, but on a candlestick; and it giveth light unto all that are in the house. Let your light so shine before men, that they may see your good works, and glorify your Father which is in heaven" (Matthew 5:14–16).

Remember Peter, the one who tried to hide the fact that he was one of Jesus' disciples? His changed behavior after the Holy Ghost came upon him at Pentecost is a model of Christian honesty and forthrightness. Following their arrest in Jerusalem, Peter and John were commanded not to speak or teach in the Name of Jesus. They answered, "Whether it be right in the sight of God to hearken unto you more than unto God, judge ye. For we cannot but speak the things which we have seen and heard" (Acts 4:19, 20).

We are not to be a hidden people or even a people who can slip into hiding when things, to the carnal mind, seem hard to bear. We are to stand out in thick and thin.

A Christian has no desire to hide his identity or to pretend to be other than he is. He is born again; this time of incorruptible seed. The old man is crucified with Christ: "Lie not one to another, seeing that ye have put off the old man with his deeds" (Colossians 3:9).

There is no guile in the mouth of a Christian—he is without fault before the Lord. But all liars shall have their part in the lake of fire (Revelation 14:5; 21:8).

One can try spiritual camouflage or mimicry and sometimes fool men, but God is never fooled. Ananias and Sapphira, seeking the favor of men, mimicked the selflessness of other Christians, but God was not deceived. Whatever else Ananias and Sapphira may have lacked, one thing is clear: they lacked faith in God as a rewarder of them who diligently seek Him. Had they lived by faith they could even have retained their property and God would have blessed their lives. Said Peter, "Whiles it remained, was it not thine own? and after it was sold, was it not in thine own power? why hast thou conceived this thing in thine heart? thou hast not lied unto men, but unto God" (Acts 5:4). However, Ananias and Sapphira did not live by faith but by appearances, and they were destroyed.

If we are tempted to pretense, or even to blend with the world, we must remember Peter's question: "Why hast thou conceived this thing in thine heart?" and this fact: "All things are naked and opened unto the eyes of him with whom we have to do" (Hebrews 4:13). God will be neither mocked nor avoided. Deception before God did not work for the first man and woman (Genesis 3), and it will not work for you and me.

Chapter 13

THE NORTH AMERICAN DESERT

Hope

How lifeless is the desert, really?

After one gets used to the continual sunshine and the clear weather becomes monotonous, the desert can seem a hopeless place. From the relatively cool, sagebrush-dominated Great Basin Desert to the hot cactus forests of the Sonoran Desert, the rule is dry weather and then . . . more dry weather. Indeed, one may be inclined to think that were the creatures of the deserts given a choice, they would elect to live elsewhere.

But this is not the case. The desert is not a hopeless place. Rather, it is a land that in a figurative sense lies waiting in *hope*—a hope that is

LEARNING FROM THE BOOK OF NATURE

always fulfilled. We who live in areas where cold grips the land each winter might typify *hope* as, snowblanketed, leafless woods slumbering in expectation of spring. However, because of the starkness of the desert landscape and the rapid response of its plants and animals to seasonal moisture, a desert's long wait for rain provides an even more striking symbol of hope.

There are two ways that plants survive desert life. One way is to exist as *perennials.* Another way is to survive as *annuals*, which grow quickly, produce seed, and then die the same year. Let us first consider the desert perennials, wonderful in themselves, before discussing the marvel of the colorful desert annuals.

THE DESERT PERENNIALS

Perennials are the plants that always seem to be there. A traveler over the Great Basin Desert any time of year sees endless vistas across sagebrush-covered land. Traveling south onto the lower-elevation Mojave Desert, he sees mile after mile of creosote bush and, in certain areas, the shaggy profiles of Joshua trees. Turning east (going lower yet in elevation) into the Sonoran Desert, he finds cactuses in multitudes and in

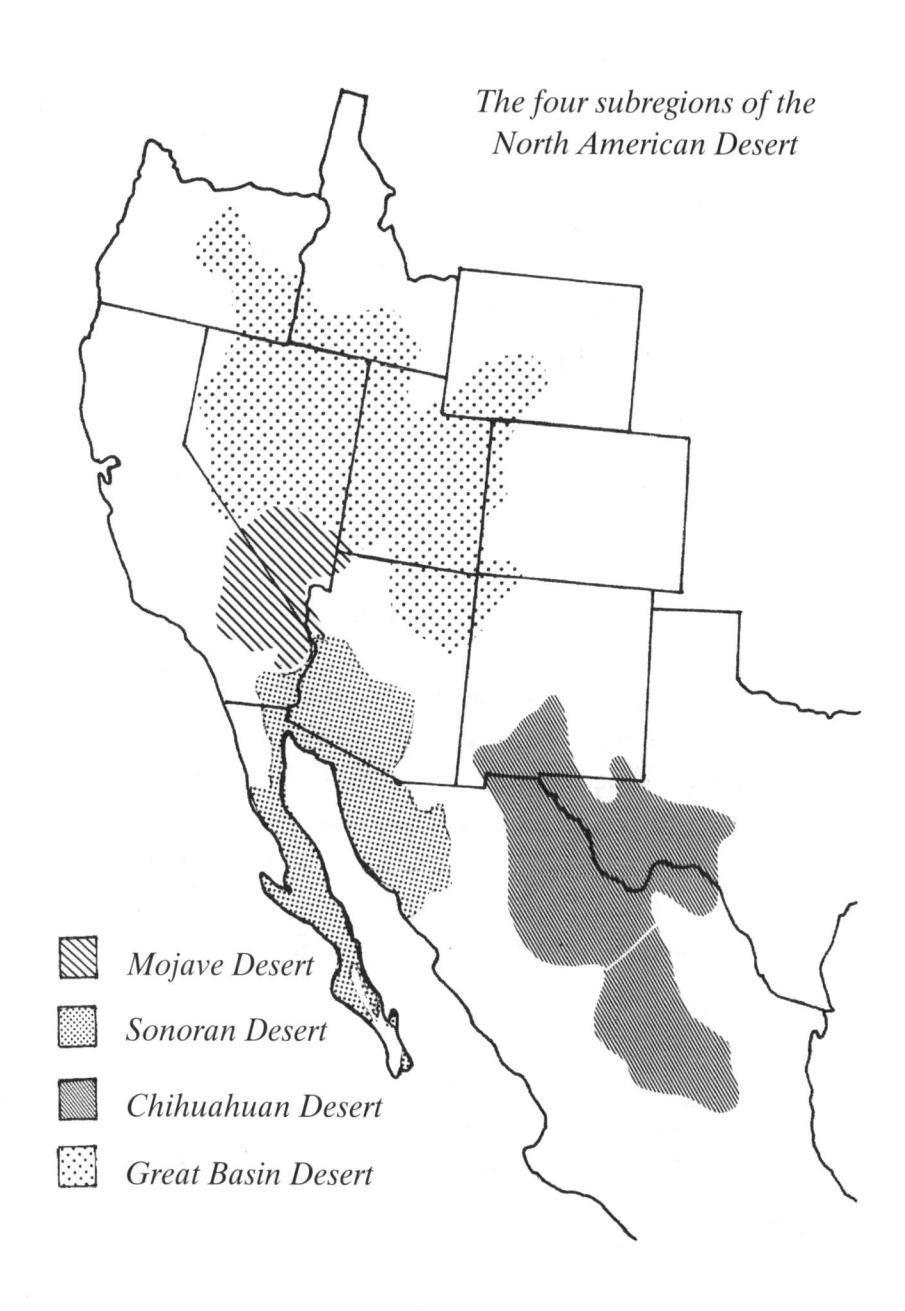

*The four subregions of the
North American Desert*

- Mojave Desert
- Sonoran Desert
- Chihuahuan Desert
- Great Basin Desert

various shapes and sizes, plus green-barked palo verde trees highlighting the courses of gravelly washes. Then farther east on the Chihuahuan Desert, where elevation is again higher and climate somewhat cooler, he observes sword-leaved yuccas, bristling prickly pear and cholla cactuses, and ice-pick-tipped agave.

These descriptions of North America's four desert regions name but a few of their most prominent perennial plants. The complete list of desert perennials is extensive, and each kind of plant has its own testimony of its Maker and Sustainer's provision for its survival. We list but a very few examples.

- The *saguaro*, fifty-foot giant of the cactus family, stores a great volume of water. During times of abundant moisture, over 80 percent of its ten-ton mass may be water.
- Roots of *mesquite*, a common desert shrub that grows nearly to tree form along washes, may penetrate into the earth one hundred feet to obtain water.
- The thorny *ocotillo* grows leaves during times of optimum moisture, but sheds them during the onset of drought.
- Night-blooming *cereus* has unimpressive stems

The North American Desert

but possesses a moisture-storing tap root that can swell to over forty pounds.
- Resembling a giant, upside-down root of wild carrot, the *boojum tree* of Sonora and Baja California has short, unforked branches with tiny leaves that offer little surface area to the threat of drying winds.
- *Creosote bush* reduces competition from other plants by giving off a chemical into its root zone that prevents their growth.

The desert perennials persist in the arid environment as standing plants, growing and flowering in the relatively short times of adequate moisture; but battened down and reinforced during the long periods of stressful desert life, waiting for the next time it rains.

THE DESERT ANNUALS

However, when the desert really "blooms," it is the annuals that contribute most to this impressive floral display. How they wait for months or even years as seeds, and then grow, bloom, fruit, and die in a rush is for them a matter of survival, but to us it is a miracle and a spectacle of beauty. It is their survival as mere tiny seeds through long periods of inadequate moisture that we will consider now.

When soil moisture is sufficient, the desert bursts into bloom. Bright yellow poppies, purple lupine, white primroses, lavender verbena, scarlet penstemon—the beauty of these annual flowers is highlighted all the more by the severity of the surrounding landscape.

There is really little difference between the appearance and structure of these desert flowers and similar annual flowers of humid areas, but the desert annuals are quite different in their pattern of life. The desert annual's seed is the focus of this difference, and dormancy is the key to the seed's survival through the long dry periods.

The seeds of desert annuals are very conservative in their response to soil moisture. They respond very little to mere ground water because it lacks the acidity needed to leach dormancy-enforcing, growth-inhibiting chemicals out of their seed coats. If they were to germinate after only a brief shower, the seedlings would wither before they could grow to produce more seed. Rainfall must be of correct timing and amount to leach the growth inhibitors out of the seed, or the seed will not respond. Another amazing thing is that the seeds of some desert annuals are capable of replacing the growth inhibitor that may be leached from their seed coats by rainfall that is insufficient to enable germinated seeds to grow into mature plants.

Because it is generally warm and rainfall comes to the Sonoran Desert twice a year, this area of the North American Desert has two seasons of bloom, winter and summer. In the Sonoran Desert, temperature works together with rain to cause germination. The seeds of annuals that bloom in winter respond to cool rains; those that bloom in summer respond only to warm rains.

Moisture is the greatest limiting factor to plant growth in the desert. Soils are relatively fertile because rainfall has not leached out nutrients. Except at the extremes, temperatures would be favorable to plant growth. Sunlight is in great supply. So when soil moisture is adequate—and when it is, this period lasts only six to eight weeks—desert annuals progress quickly through their cycle of growth.

DESERT CREATURES

The result in the years when there is ample moisture is not only a marvelous display of natural color, but also an overabundance of seeds.

This is not by accident—it is by design. Seed-eating animals and their predators need to survive too. The Lord provides for them in this bounty of seeds from the annuals. Thus, the desert animals also have much to accomplish during these periods of abundant rain.

Along with the sudden return of the desert annuals comes a dramatic increase in the population of the insects that pollinate them, and along with this rapid increase in insect life comes a rush of activity among the animals that eat the insects. All these seeming population explosions—flowers, insects, and insect eaters—are the normal periodic responses of desert life to rain.

The *spadefoot* toad, for example, stays buried beneath the surface of the Sonoran Desert during the driest ten months of the year. Then during the moist period it busies itself in two months of activity above the ground.

Puddles are to the spadefoot toad what nests are to birds; it must have them to reproduce its kind. After a heavy rain, spadefoots are legion, gathering at puddles along the washes to lay their eggs.

When a transitory toad must lay its eggs in a

The North American Desert

temporary puddle along a drying desert streambed, development of the young has to progress rapidly. Eggs hatch into tadpoles in from 1 1/2 to 3 days. In a little over a month the tadpoles become toads, ready to feed on the population of insects also recently increased by the rains.

In their two months of activity along the desert washes, the spadefoot toads fulfill their Creator's plan for their fruitfulness. Then, having multiplied their kind, with return of dry weather, the spadefoot toads use the spurs on their hind feet to dig themselves backwards into the soil. Having buried themselves, they return to an inactive state, conserving their bodies' water for survival till the short rainy season next year.

The lives of desert birds are also affected by the seasonal rain. Some habits of some kinds of birds are so harmonized with the abundance of insects following rain that these birds will mate and nest only after the rain has arrived. Then within a week, nests may be built and filled with their complement of eggs.

The desert is a land of hope—a hope that is always fulfilled. The Lord always *does* send rain. God, who cannot lie, made this promise: "While the earth remaineth, seedtime and harvest, and cold and heat, and summer and winter, and day and night shall not cease" (Genesis 8:22).

OUR LIVING HOPE

Life looks like a desert to people lacking Jesus in their hearts. Many of these work to find ways to irrigate their own deserts, and often they succeed for a time. With riches, play, education, reputation, comfort, and other fleeting things, they cover the real dryness of their lives.

But all that it takes to reveal the real desert that underlies their efforts is for their personal resources to dry up. Wealth and health can be lost, and comfort with them. Education can become outdated. Reputation can be tarnished. One thing about a lush, irrigated desert: all we have to do is stop applying water and it rapidly becomes arid again, often all the uglier for our temporary watering.

Life in Christ is not like that. In Jesus, God provides refreshing showers of blessing that save men from the dryness that is due to sin. Through God's abundant provision, these redeemed people bloom and grow. They even come to reproduce themselves, because God works through them to water the arid souls of others. God promised this productivity.

"And if thou draw out thy soul to the hungry, and satisfy the afflicted soul; then shall thy light rise in obscurity, and thy darkness be as the noonday: and the Lord shall guide thee continually, and satisfy thy soul in drought, and make fat thy bones: and thou shalt be like a watered garden, and like a spring of water, whose waters fail not" (Isaiah 58:10, 11).

As he lives in Christ, and for Him, the Christian often faces very trying times—times when temptation comes to him to see life as being very dry. God's abundant provisions will carry us through such times. In fact, when our lives are driest and harshest by outward standards, then will God's supply of blessing be most precious to us.

As we observe unconverted people, we see people with very little hope. Perhaps this explains why they strive so much with one another about personal rights and the satisfaction of immediate wants. Seeing this hopelessness and the strife it generates in a person's soul, we recognize that one of the sweetest blessings that God showers on His children is hope.

As we have seen, the desert is not a hopeless place, but a place that in a figurative sense lies waiting *in* hope. Neither is life a hopeless thing.

First, God assures hope for all men. Jesus came "that they might have life, and that they might have it more abundantly" (John 10:10). He came that all men might be saved (John 10:9).

Second, there is a special hope for the Christian. We can hope in God because He is "the God of hope" (Romans 15:13). God will strengthen us to be faithful to His commands in this life and will take the faithful into His eternal presence in the next. We say "amen" to the Twenty-third Psalm, a meditation of David, for we know our hope will be fulfilled.

"The Lord is my shepherd; I shall not want. He maketh me to lie down in green pastures: he leadeth me beside the still waters. He restoreth my soul: he leadeth me in the paths of righteousness for his name's sake. Yea, though I walk through the valley of the shadow of death, I will fear no evil: for thou art with me; thy rod and thy staff they comfort me. Thou preparest a table before me in the presence of mine enemies: thou anointest my head with oil; my cup runneth over. Surely goodness and mercy shall follow me all the days of my life: and I will dwell in the house of the Lord for ever" (Psalm 23).

> Life is not a desert sere
> When Christ is near:
> Christ in us, the hope of glory.

Chapter 14

INSECT PESTS AND SOLENODON

It Seemed Like a Good Idea

How can we know if our ideas truly are good ones?

It seemed like a good idea at first. Then after they had actually tried it, it seemed like a *very* good idea. The insect pests attacking fields of the farmers in the Matamoros-Reynosa area in northeastern Mexico had seriously reduced the cotton yields. The control of these insects with increasingly intensive use of pesticides seemed well worth the cost.

Then, in just a few years, insect damage to the cotton crop far exceeded that inflicted before the initiation of heavier pesticide applications.

Things got so bad that cotton-growing acreage dropped from 710,000 acres in 1960 to 1,200 acres in 1970. Meanwhile, the pesticide-intensive cotton farming shifted two hundred miles south to the Tampico-Monte area, where 500,000 acres were planted in 1966. However, due to increasing damage by insects, in just four years the production of cotton was limited to 1,200 acres there too.

What happened to make such a good idea turn into such a bad one? The natural balance among the insects living in and around the cotton fields was repeatedly upset by the heavy and frequent applications of chemical pesticides. Unexpectedly, in the rebound following the treatments, the reproduction of the types of insects that were hungry for cotton was so intense that the Mexican cotton industry was practically eliminated.

*　　　*　　　*　　　*　　　*

Native to the islands of Cuba and Haiti are two kinds of a small animal called *solenodon*. These creatures are ratlike in appearance—two feet long, including the tail and having beady eyes. Also, they have a very long, whiskered snout

Cuban solenodon

LEARNING FROM THE BOOK OF NATURE

that is useful for rooting in the soil in their nighttime searches for insects. Not a pretty animal, but still one that has a useful role in the corner of the world where God placed it.

Today, the solenodon is a rare creature; its existence is considered endangered. This was not always so, but when the *mongoose*—a small, weasel-like predator—was imported to these islands to control rats and snakes, it also began killing the solenodon and many other small furbearers and birds. Mongooses have become a threat to the population of small animals wherever they are introduced. Consequently, what seemed like a good idea has backfired.

The Bible records many examples of "good ideas" among the people who lived during centuries past that were poorly thought out—or not thought out at all. The consequences were always regrettable and often disastrous. We will mention only a few of these cases.

Consider the consequences of Adam and Eve's actions based on the ideas introduced to them by the serpent; or the results of Lot's decision to dwell in the cities of the plain; or the events following Dinah's venture out to see the daughters of the land of Shechem.

Insect Pests and Solenodon

One example among many of the troubles that self-seeking ideas consistently brought the Israelites during their forty years in the wilderness was the rebellion of Korah and his company against the authority of Moses. It may have seemed like a good idea, at first.

In the time of the kings, Saul thought it good to disobey God when he kept the best of the flocks of the Amalekites as a bounty of war and spared the life of King Agag as a sign of victory.

David thought it would be satisfying to commit adultery with Bathsheba.

Zedekiah believed it advantageous to ignore God's word through the prophet Jeremiah.

During the life of Jesus, the Pharisees considered their attempts to silence Him as acts of righteousness. The chief priests called it civic responsibility to seek His death, and Judas sought personal advantage in betraying Him. Early in the life of the New Testament church, Ananias and his wife, Sapphira, thought it to their personal good to hold back part of their estate from the welfare of the brotherhood while professing to give it all.

God's Word tells us of the sad and often terrible outcomes of these ideas that seemed good to man but bad to God. If only they had received with meekness "the engrafted word." The apostle James wrote that it is able to save men's souls. How much more easily could it have saved them from earthly peril and tragedy?

The tendency continues today, however, for men to be only hearers of the Word, and not doers. Like Dinah, young people may have an idea that seems good to them and, perhaps, to their friends, but that is contrary to the judgment and desires of their parents. Followers of Christ may decide that they will turn and pursue their own "good ideas." Rather, they should obey God's Word: it tells children to obey their parents in the Lord, and is right at hand to guide and reprove the Christian.

The Bible warns those who base their actions only on what seems right to them: "There is a way which seemeth right unto a man, but the end thereof are the ways of death" (Proverbs 14:12). In contrast, the Bible admonishes us, "Trust in the Lord with all thine heart; and lean not unto thine own understanding. In all thy ways acknowledge him, and he shall direct thy paths" (Proverbs 3:5, 6).

Only as our ideas are in harmony with the

Word can we be confident that they will be truly good ones.

"For ever, O Lord, thy word is settled in heaven.

"Teach me, O Lord, the way of thy statutes; and I will keep it unto the end."

Psalm 119:33, 89

Chapter 15

ANT, HORNBILL, SALMON, AND BEAVER

Insects, Fowls, Beasts, and the Sluggard

What can these four diverse kinds of animals teach about daily living?

King Solomon "was wiser than all men" (1 Kings 4:31). He spoke three thousand proverbs. No doubt his proverbs included a number of illustrations from nature, for "he spake of trees, from the cedar tree that is in Lebanon even unto the hyssop that springeth out of the wall: he spake also of beasts, and of fowl, and of creeping things, and of fishes" (1 Kings 4:33).

Whichever character quality we consider, we find numerous examples of that quality among God's "beasts, . . . fowl, . . . creeping things, . . . and . . . fishes."

From God's grand array of animals, we will select four of His creatures that illustrate qualities of industry and perseverance.

THE CREEPING THINGS

The creature of God's handiwork that Solomon chose to contrast industry and perseverance with laziness and inattention was the tiny *ant*, one of the *creeping things*. We will let the Scriptures speak for themselves on the lesson to be learned from these little insects.

"Go to the ant, thou sluggard; consider her ways, and be wise: which having no guide, overseer, or ruler, provideth her meat in the summer, and gathereth her food in the harvest. How long wilt thou sleep, O sluggard? when wilt thou arise out of thy sleep? Yet a little sleep, a little slumber, a little folding of the hands to sleep: so shall thy poverty come as one that travelleth, and thy want as an armed man" (Proverbs 6:6–11).

THE FOWL

We will also consider the perseverance and industry of a *fowl*, the *hornbill* of the African and Asian tropics. The male hornbill is responsible

A great hornbill feeds his mate through a slit left in the mud wall she built over the entrance of their nesting cavity.

for feeding both his mate and their young during the nesting period. Before she begins laying, the female hornbill enters a cavity, such as a hollow in a tree, and the male brings her mud and other materials with which she seals herself inside. She leaves only a slit through which he can pass the great quantity of food that he so dedicatedly gathers during the weeks of her confinement.

THE FISHES

The migratory *salmon* of the Pacific Ocean are *fishes* illustrating the virtue of steadfast effort. Salmon hatch from eggs laid in nests on gravelly, freshwater streambeds. Sooner or later they swim downstream to the ocean through waters dangerous with predators and, in recent decades, pollution and man's impoundments—dams backing up water for miles and miles. Depending on the location of the stream and the kind of salmon, their trip may be short, or it may cover two thousand miles. If a salmon safely reaches its destination, the salt water, it may over the next several years, travel more thousands of miles in the ocean.

In their appointed time, however, salmon return to the mouth of their home river system and begin the exhausting trip upstream, back to their birthplace. It is at this time, when the fish are "running," that commercial and amateur fishermen diminish salmon numbers. Those that escape the fisherman pass on, back to familiar waters—through the salty, the fresh, the flowing, the polluted, and the impounded.

At many of the reservoirs, men have built *fish ladders* to allow the salmon to continue upstream around the dams. However, these artificial waterfalls require exertion beyond that for which the salmon were designed. Many die short of their destination.

When the salmon begin their journey upstream, they cease eating (even though they may strike at fishermen's artificial lures) and live off stored fat. Unchangeably intent on their destination, they drive against the flowing waters, bound through rushing rapids, and leap to the top of waterfalls up to ten feet high.

When successful ones reach the stream of their birth, they spawn. Then, like their parents before them, they linger on a short time and die. But in their persistent hard work, they accomplish their Creator's goal for their migration: the reproduction of their kind.

THE BEASTS

Because of the *beaver's* uniqueness, the references in literature to this *beast* are numerous. Its natural industry and perseverance have long impressed and fascinated man. Even today, in our urbanized world, those who have never seen a wild beaver at work may use the clichés "eager beaver" or "busy beaver" to refer to an energetic worker.

The anatomy of the beaver is, in itself, a catalog of marvelously designed and constructed tools. The tail is a rudder for steering, a support during tree-felling, and an alarm-maker to signal danger to the beaver colony.

The front feet are clawed for excavation, and the rear feet are webbed for swimming.

The front teeth grow throughout the beaver's life—his daily gnawing on wood will not wear them out.

Flaps behind these front teeth close off the rear part of the mouth to water and wood chips, except at mealtime.

Tiny ears and nostrils are easily sealed to exclude water during swimming.

An inner eyelid is transparent, closing over

the eye underwater but still allowing the beaver to see.

The fur is designed to trap air, suitably insulative against even freezing waters.

The Designer was not concerned only with the *mechanics* of equipping His creature, however. The beaver, therefore, has a disposition (by design) that suits him to use these marvelous tools with complete competency.

There are no lost moments or motions for the industrious beaver, and *perseverance* is the word for its engineering endeavors. It gnaws away at a tree until the tree topples, and then systematically cuts off the branches. The log and branches are then transported to the water—they are food and building materials to the beaver.

If beavers are working away from the banks of the water, they may dig canals, sometimes over two hundred yards long, for floating logs to their impoundment. Their dam is built of logs, branches, and stones, with mud for mortar, and may be maintained for years.

The beaver family is housed in a lodge that is built and maintained with the same techniques used on the dam. The lodge stands in the water with its entrances underwater. It protects the beaver family in its comings and goings and permits easy access in winter to their underwater food stores.

When you are casting about for an illustration for some particular Christian character quality, go to the beasts, or fowls, or creeping things, or fishes. You will be following the lead of a very wise man.

"The mighty God, even the Lord, hath spoken and called the earth from the rising of the sun unto the going down thereof. . . .

"Every beast of the forest is mine, and the cattle upon a thousand hills.

"I know all the fowls of the mountains: and the wild beasts of the field are mine."

Psalm 50:1, 10, 11

Chapter 16

ALARMING OCCURRENCES

Frightening Things Also Declare the Glory of God

What do we do when nature makes us afraid?

"Let the heavens rejoice, and let the earth be glad: let the sea roar, and the fulness thereof. Let the field be joyful, and all that is therein: then shall all the trees of the wood rejoice before the Lord" (Psalm 96:11–13).

We read Psalm 96 in family worship this morning, and I was especially impressed by one aspect of verses 11–13. We who recognize God as the Creator are accustomed to thinking of the heavens as declaring the glory of God, of spring's fragrant growth as symbolic of the spiritual regeneration that is in Christ, of the complex functioning of our bodies as the work of His fearful and wonderful intelligence, and so on.

Yet when we read the latter part of verse 11 during family worship—"let the sea roar"—I wondered if we do not fall short of perceiving that the frightening and eerie things in nature are also intended by God to stimulate an attitude of rejoicing in His children.

I know that one can stand on the margin of the ocean and become melancholy, or even frightened, in thinking of the vastness of the deep and the unrelenting, countless breakers that roll in and crash against the shore. Yet the Word of God says, "Let the heavens rejoice, and let the earth be glad; let the sea *roar*, and the fulness thereof."

Often have my wife or I been called to our children's rooms during a late night's thunderstorm. Little ones can be terrified at times by the flashing lightning and jarring thunder. Let us comfort our fearful children, while we ourselves rejoice in the power and might of the Creator, as His Word instructs us.

How much easier it is for us to dwell on verse 12 (which is also true) of the psalm than to take

Alarming Occurrences

hold of the idea behind "let the sea roar, and the fulness thereof." The gentler things of nature—a hummingbird flitting among the blossoms, a cottontail nibbling clover, or a quiet sunrise after a moonlit night—are much more to our liking than is a roaring tiger, a rending earthquake, or an erupting volcano. Yet all reflect God's power, and we can only rejoice in that.

However, it is not only in attitudes toward such frightful occurrences as tornadoes and avalanches or such fearsome creatures as sharks and crocodiles that we may fall short of perceiving nature as something to rejoice about. Some people are unreasonably fearful of tiny harmless creatures, fleeing from a room at the sight of a mouse or abandoning a yard to an eighteen-inch garter snake. Friends, trap the mouse and drive off the snake, but even then take time to rejoice at the glory of their Creator. They are not so fearfully and wonderfully made as you are, but they are still amazing evidence of the Lord's handiwork.

Far worse than fright—certainly there is a place for being startled into good judgment—is the superstitiousness with which some people relate to nature. Superstition is not for Christians.

One Lord's Day a few years ago my wife and an older sister in Christ walked up our hollow to visit the women in a family new to our neighborhood. Our hollow abounded in bird life, and one thing we greatly enjoyed each evening was the call of the whippoorwills up and down the narrow valley. This simple pleasure was mentioned in the course of the visit. The wife and mother of the family new to our hollow stated that the song of the whippoorwills was "spooky" to her; it made her think that someone was going to die soon. In response to this the older sister said, "Oh, when I hear them call 'whip-poor-will,' I like to think they are saying, 'Praise the Lord! Praise the Lord!'"

I appreciate this sister's viewpoint, and I believe it is the correct way to look at God's creation: "Let the heavens rejoice . . . let the earth be glad . . . let the sea roar. . . let the field be joyful, and all that is therein." I think her viewpoint is Scriptural in at least three ways.

First, she recognized that the creation praises its Maker (Psalm 19:1).

Second, "whatsoever things are true, whatsoever things are honest, whatsoever things are just, whatsoever things are pure, whatsoever things are lovely, whatsoever things are of good report; . . . if there be any praise" (Philippians 4:8)—she thought on these things.

Third, she girded up the loins of her mind (1 Peter 1:13). That is, she resisted superstition *and* false wisdom. To the superstitious the falsely wise might say, "Well, it's just a bird, and it has its own call so that it can attract or warn other birds like it."

Reader, gird up the loins of *your* mind. Do not deny yourself the great blessing of appreciating all nature as the Lord's creation.

Chapter 17

ADOPTION IN NATURE

God the Father and Joseph the Father—of Jesus

What is God's view of adoption?

The natural affection of the people of God for children and the frequent lack of it among the people of the world contrast distinctly. The Bible presents a specific case that heightens this contrast. It is the account in Matthew of the adoption of God's Son, Jesus, by Joseph.

I trust this idea of Joseph adopting the Son of God will not seem irreverent, for it gives insight into both Joseph's vision of the kingdom of God and His willingness to serve his heavenly Father. It is apparent from the Scriptures that Joseph could have legally and conscientiously separated from Mary, his betrothed. Rather, he accepted her and took her baby, Jesus, to raise as his own son. Also, considering the later testimony of Jesus' life, we are convinced that Joseph's devotion to fatherhood was not lukewarm; Joseph was a good father to Jesus. God chose Joseph for this responsibility; God makes good choices.

Adoption obviously had a place in God's sight: He chose it for His own Son, selecting Joseph of Nazareth to fulfill the role of adoptive father. There is further powerful Bible evidence of God's acceptance of adoption. "When the fulness of time was come, God sent forth his Son, made of a woman, made under the law, to redeem them that were under the law, that we might receive the adoption of sons" (Galatians 4:4, 5).

Praise God! If we are among the redeemed, we are His adopted sons. But the blessing does not stop there—read on to Galatians 4:6. "And because ye are sons, God hath sent forth the Spirit of his Son into your hearts, crying, Abba, Father." So, in God's sight an *adopted* son is a *real* son. God does not hold back any of His love from me merely because I was once *not* His son, and I can now approach Him with complete trust in His tender love.

There is reluctance by some to think of adopted children as the "real" children of the parents who adopted them. Likewise there is a tendency to fail to accept adoptive parents as the "real" parents of adopted children.

These are not correct views. God was willing to have His Son adopted, and He opened the way for our spiritual adoption as sons. Further, there is the witness of adoptive parents. They testify to the same high level of love for their adopted children that they have (or would have) for children born to them.

I see the adoptive father and mother as further, somewhat distinctive, evidence of the God-given desire of men and women to express parental love. Of course, we have heard sad stories of adoptive parents who oppressed their child with the impression that he or she is a poor substitute for a "real" child. And sometimes we hear of an adopted child who later rebels against the thought of being adopted. He may think, "What's wrong with me? Where are my real parents?" One way or another, in both cases these unhappy people received the wrong impression of what adoption means. It should mean to us what it means to God: it is an acceptable—and real—way for God to bring children into a good family situation.

We end this essay with a lesson from the Book of Nature. There are many examples on the farm of female animals adopting young. It is a common practice to set broody hens on the eggs of less dependable sitters such as ducks, guinea fowl, and turkeys. The hen may begin acting a little distracted if, as in the case of duck eggs, she has to sit longer than her normal twenty-one days; but when the eggs hatch she will try to mother the strange little ones as if they were chicks. When a rabbit grower recognizes a doe that is particularly receptive to adopting bunnies from outside her litter, he will keep her around for just that purpose. Orphaned calves are often taken to cows who will accept them and allow them to nurse. However, one of the most interesting cases I know of adoption by a domestic animal occurred last summer with one of our neighbor's cats.

A neighbor had found a box of very small kittens sitting along the road. She distributed the little things around the neighborhood, but before long we could see that the two we got were not

Adoption in Nature

going to make it without the care of a mother cat. Another neighbor had also accepted two, and we heard that they were taking theirs to one of their mother cats who was still nursing her half-grown litter. She did not show a great deal of interest in the newcomers, but she would nurse them if forced to lie still. So we took our two there.

Getting an unwilling mother cat to lie still for *four* new kittens turned out to be too great a challenge, so our neighbor's girls began hand-feeding them. This had not worked for us earlier with our two, so we thought it probably would fail again.

Then something unusual happened. When one of the girls went to feed the four kittens, they were missing. Searching farther, she found that a kittenless female cat had taken an interest in them and made a nest for them. Even though the kittens were unable to get nourishment from her, still the cat was otherwise mothering them. Each time the girl finished feeding the kittens, the adoptive mother cat would carry them back to her nest.

The interesting thing is, those kittens that had looked like emaciated starvelings began to perk up and fill out. Our neighbor feels it was really because of that dry (no milk) mother cat. He says there was really nothing so special about that cow's milk—many orphan kittens have died on just such a diet. It did fill a need, but still he is convinced it was a dry cat's desire to be a mother that made the difference.

At any rate, we have concrete evidence of this success story. Her name is Pansy, and I think right now she is probably sleeping in a sunny window in the barn.

Genuine mothering worked wonders.

"For as many as are led by the Spirit of God, they are the sons of God.

"For . . . ye have received the Spirit of adoption, whereby we cry, Abba, Father.

"The Spirit itself beareth witness with our spirit, that we are the children of God:

"And if children, then heirs; heirs of God, and joint heirs with Christ."

Romans 8:14–17

Chapter 18

THE DOMESTIC HEN

The Example of a Mother Hen

What does any good mother want her little ones to do when she calls for them to come? How does that remind us of God our Father?

"O Jerusalem, Jerusalem, which killest the prophets, and stonest them that are sent unto thee; how often would I have gathered thy children together, as a hen doth gather her brood under her wings, and ye would not!" (Luke 13:34).

Did Jesus lower the quality of His love for Israel when He compared Himself to a mother hen? We are sure He did not.

*   *   *   *   *

LEARNING FROM THE BOOK OF NATURE

Last summer one of our buff hens was broody, so we set a dozen eggs under her. Twenty-one days later her patience was rewarded with twelve peeping yellow chicks. As the little ones began hatching, the hen's long, stolid silence changed to anxious clucking. Even before her tiny nestlings broke through their shells, mother hen was already calling to them, encouraging them in their efforts.

A little later when the chicks were hatched and dry, they began poking their heads out from under their mother's feathery body. It was our children's earnest interest to count them. This made the nervous mother hen almost frantic; any finger pointing too close was a target for attempted pecking.

For several weeks we enjoyed watching biddy lead her little flock around the barnyard. The best was none too good for her chicks. Though the hen fed herself too, discovery of any particularly nutritious morsel set her to clucking for them to come. They always came running, and their faithful mother directed their attention to the bit of choice food with a *cluck, cluck, cluck* and the scratching of her feet.

At any suspicion of danger, an alarmed sort

of clucking drew the little chicks quickly to their mother, who invited them to take refuge under her wings. The hen always kept her chicks a safe distance from the rest of the flock and returned them to the barn before the other chickens went in to roost at the end of the day. Every evening well before sunset she was settled back on her nest in the northeast corner of the barn, her brood secure beneath her.

*   *   *   *   *

Scientists point out that it is not good to ascribe man's characteristics and qualities to nature. This is largely true. Ascribing man's characteristics and qualities to animals (some would even stretch them to include plants) soon leads to foolish sentimentalism, and the Lord has much more important things for us to reflect on.

On the other hand, God has lessons for us in nature, and we are required to compare ourselves to a number of different things in the creation. If we did not, we could not understand parts of the written Word.

The ants, conies, locusts, and spider of Proverbs 30:24–28 are four examples. The hen and chicks of Luke 13:34 is another. Indeed, the

LEARNING FROM THE BOOK OF NATURE

Lord was not hesitant to use the behavior of that humble creature, the domestic hen, to reveal something of Himself.

In Christ's comparison of Himself to a mother hen and Israel to her chicks, our mental picture is one of unaffected, unpretentious, self-sacrificing love. It is the kind of love that does not merely *share*—it *gives*. It is the sort of love that assumes the necessity of an obedient response, not because it is impressed with its own power to require obedience, but because it always knows what is best.

Then also, this illustration inclines us to think of motherhood at its finest, when Mother always puts the best interests of her children before her own. How warming the memory of a loving mother is to her grown-up children! How reassuring the sheltering arms of a comforting mother are to her little ones!

Nature is replete with examples of animal mothers devoted to the care of their young. The mother *bear* senses danger and sends her cubs scrambling up a tree to safety. At an alarmed cry from their mother, *spotted sandpiper* chicks crouch to the ground and lie motionless. Later another call signals them to come to the shelter

The Domestic Hen

of Mother's wings. The *grouse* hen leads enemies away from its chicks by feigning a broken wing.

There are also devoted mothers among kinds of animals we might not expect to show such devotion. During her nesting period the female *crocodile* is a steadfast mother. She must be vigilant. She leaves her earthen nest only briefly, to eat or to cool off a little. Various creatures relish crocodile eggs, and the several dozen she lays would soon be devoured if she left her nest for long. She sits on guard for three months, waiting as the sun-warmed earth incubates her eggs.

When at last she hears her babies call from inside the eggs, she digs into the nest. Gathering the hatching brood into her fearsome jaws, she carries them to the greater safety of their watery nursery. These are critical moments in the life of a crocodile, for some of the same predators that would have devoured it in the egg might be lingering by now, ready to snatch it up as a foot-long hatchling. Those successfully transported in their mother's mouth from nest to nursery are guarded by both parents for several weeks as they grow and learn to fend for themselves.

Cichlids are fish that mate for life. The care

of these simple fish for their young is extraordinarily like the care men and women *should* give to their children.

There are about six hundred different kinds of cichlids, and there is some variation in the way the different ones care for their young. The following paragraphs are a generalized description of the parental behavior of the kinds of cichlids that spawn and tend their young on stream and lake bottoms.

Before their small fry ever hatch, cichlid parents are always near the incubation nest, periodically relieving one another to fan a steady stream of fresh water past their eggs. They continue fanning after their tiny baby fish have been moved, by mouth, to a fresh nest site. The cleanliness and health of their young are important to cichlid parents. When the little cichlids are able to swim, father and mother are there to guard them as they move about the neighborhood.

At evening the parents gather their young back into the nest. Mother hovers above it, signaling with her fins, "Assemble below." Father meanwhile faithfully scours the area for lost or wandering offspring, collecting them in his mouth, delivering them home, and blowing them into the nest hollow.

Such a well-wrought analogy of animal behavior to Christian parenthood can only be the work of the wise Creator, who uses His creation to instruct us.

"Ask now the beasts, and they shall teach thee; and the fowls of the air, and they shall tell thee: or speak to the earth, and it shall teach thee: and the fishes of the sea shall declare unto thee. Who knoweth not in all these that the hand of the Lord hath wrought this?" (Job 12:7–9).

* * * * *

Jenny was a very friendly cow. That is, she was very friendly when all she had was us. After she had her calf, she became a stranger to us. But at least we always knew where to find her and her baby—at the far end of the pasture, as close to the line fence as she could get.

The third day after her calf was born I went out to bring the two of them in to the barn, but her calf was gone. There stood the cow, placidly grazing, but no calf. I walked around and around the pasture, and as I walked I felt increasingly foolish. After all, the grass was so short that even a snake could have spotted a reclining calf.

Next I decided to go under the fence into the neighbor's hayfield to see if somehow the calf had gotten over there and died. The hay was overgrown, and I had to search the field in narrow sweeps so as not to miss anything. Meanwhile Jenny continued calmly grazing, showing no concern for her missing calf.

Back and forth I went. Suddenly I saw Jenny's head swing up and her ears go erect. Then her legs and her voice both went into action, and she hurried toward the fence, mooing anxiously. Just ahead of me, her calf rose quickly to her feet—not so agile as her mother, but just as anxious—and "hightailed" it for the fence. Under she went, calf and mother hurrying toward one another. Jenny sniffed her over (to determine if I had abused her?), and then as quickly as a three-day-old calf could move, mother led daughter in the opposite direction from me.

The communication between that simple beast and her calf was more eloquent than many well-chosen words could have been. *I* was the one who had not understood. Motherhood needed no language.

Though the world around will not understand, we must respond to Christ as that calf responded to her mother. When the cow called, the calf arose and went. That is just what Matthew the tax collector did when Jesus said, "Follow me." He arose and followed Him.

God created chicks and calves to come when their mothers call—to them it is instinctual. To us, created in His image, He gave a will. We can decide, like Matthew, to come to Jesus when He calls. Or, like Jerusalem, we can refuse.

Let us choose to come.

"My sheep hear my voice, and I know them, and they follow me" (John 10:27).

Chapter 19

THE SUN AND ITS LIGHT

The Ecology of the Universe: Sunlight and Sonlight

How do the sun and the Son compare?

It is no wonder that most scientists of our day deny the Bible's account of the Creation, either wholly or in part. Because of unbelief, they cannot look to the Creator for illumination, and their vision is consequently nearsighted. Unless they put on the corrective lenses of faith and see that the origin of their world was as it is recorded in Genesis 1, they are set on the course described in Romans 1:18–32.

In a sense, they need to see that there is an ecology of the universe. One of their problems is that they make too much distinction between the life sciences and the physical sciences. This can be illustrated by comparing *ecology* (the study of plants and animals in relation to their surroundings) with *astronomy* (the scientific study of the celestial bodies).

Biologists who study ecology have become very good at observing and reporting on the lives and needs of plants and animals. Astronomers are compiling an impressive record of celestial occurrences and relationships. Tragically, because of failure to accept a master plan, most of them cannot see the Master Planner. The result—they cannot see the supernatural foundations of their areas of natural study. Ironically then, they are not able to even be objective—a requirement for a scientist. Rather, their very observations are warped to fit into the pattern of belief (or unbelief) of other God-ignoring men, but not into the design of God. Unless they see that there is an ecology of the universe that was started on the first day of Creation, they can never open the door to the deep and complete relationship between their two fields of study—the earth and the heavens.

An understanding of the ecology of the universe, however, opens the door to awareness of the close affinities among fields of science. This

The Sun and Its Light

awareness begins with a study of the first chapter of the Bible. It was at the Creation that God established an ecology of the universe.

The Earth and other planets in our solar system, our sun, our Milky Way galaxy, and all other galaxies existing in space are exactly where they need to be so that life can exist on planet Earth. Further, the changes occurring on a celestial scale are necessary for the balance or ecology of the universe to be maintained and for Earth to continue to exist as a home for man.

Earth's neighbor and guide, the sun, and the light that it emanates provide an inspiring illustration of the unimaginable scale and detail that God used in providing for our existence.

At the sun's core, where thermonuclear reactions occur on a scale incomparable to anything man can devise, the temperature is estimated to be 27 million degrees F. Solar prominences arch up through the corona of the sun's atmosphere 500,000 miles, moving at a speed of two hundred miles per second. (Can we fully comprehend the power of our God?) Yet here on earth 93 million miles away, we step outside on a sunny day and sigh, "M-m-m, that warm sun feels good." (Can we fully comprehend the love and mercy of our heavenly Father?)

Further, God, who gave us the sun to brighten and warm our days, had other things in mind for its service to us. It holds Earth and the other planets in its gravitational grasp as they run through their orbits. The sun controls climate and weather. Sunlight is the source of energy for the growth of plants, which feed us and our animals and provide fiber for clothing and lumber for shelter. Other plants grow to become some of our main sources of fuel.

Without sunlight, all life on earth would end. However, even if the sun were only slightly closer or farther away, the amount and nature of sunlight reaching the earth would be sufficiently different that life could not exist.

Yes, it is a universe made for man, and the sun's light is a wonderful component in God's ecology of the universe. The Scriptural record of God's spiritual relationship to light is even richer and more encouraging to the Christian than is His material creation and control of light.

Natural light shows the power of God and His love and mercy toward all men. Remember though, God only partially reveals Himself in the Book of Nature. His revelation is incomplete without the supernatural light generated by Jesus Christ (the Word become flesh), condensed in

The Sun and Its Light

the Holy Bible (the written Word), and reflected in the lives of believers (God's Holy Spirit encouraging His church).

God's Son said, "I am the light of the world: he that followeth me shall not walk in darkness, but shall have the light of life" (John 8:12). God's written "word is a lamp unto my feet, and a light unto my path" (Psalm 119:105). Jesus Christ teaches His disciples: "Ye are the light of the world. . . . Let your light so shine before men, that they may see your good works, and glorify your Father which is in heaven" (Matthew 5:14, 16).

In eternity some men will continue to see by light, but no longer by light generated by the sun. Christ's faithful ones will dwell forever in the holy city, where there will be "no need of the sun, neither of the moon, to shine in it: for the glory of God [shall] lighten it, and the Lamb is the light thereof" (Revelation 21:23).

Those who reject Christ, who turn from His light in their earthly lives, will experience eternally the outer darkness Jesus spoke of in Matthew 22:23. The light of heaven will not reach where they are; those "to whom is reserved the blackness of darkness for ever" (Jude 13). God will prepare a fire that sheds no light. When He withdraws His presence from men and the place where they abide, there will be perfect and complete darkness.

But no one need experience that dark, eternal separation from God. Until that Day of Judgment, anyone can come to Christ and receive His mercy. Oh, to be in His presence eternally, face to face, where there can be no darkness, only fulness of light!

*   *   *   *   *

There is a man-conceived ecology of this world, but a God-ordained ecology over all. Here the boundaries that man has built between the natural and the supernatural fade in the light of the Lamb, who is also the Creator.

Men who claim to see a balance of nature that they believe is the result of billions of years of chance are tragically misled. Their refusal to believe God's Word allows them to treat their beliefs about God as intellectual problems, screening out the holy light that would reveal them to be spiritual and moral problems.

We praise God that just as He continues to shine sunlight into the natural world, so He also beams Sonlight from Jesus into the darkness of men's minds that they might be saved.